The Inns of Rockport Cookbook

The Rockport Innkeepers Association

Copyright © 2019 The Rockport Innkeepers Association
Second Edition 2020
All rights reserved.
ISBN:
ISBN- 9781793422705

The Inns of Rockport Cookbook

Welcome

The Inns of Rockport welcome you to our quaint and quirky quintessential seaside village. When visiting Rockport, expect the unexpected! Surprises await you around every corner and your lodging becomes part of the adventure: imaginative chefs, period furnishings, stunning regional artwork, rocking chair porches, magical gardens, towering turrets, breathtaking ocean views, tennis courts, indoor and outdoor pools and certainly, knowledgeable innkeepers and guests with interesting stories to share.

Did you know that there are over 25 inns within our town? Each has its own unique style and personality, offering accommodations for every taste, from charming homes and cottages, colonial era inns, architectural Victorian gems and Art Deco mansions, to modern low-rise hotels and extended stay properties. When you stay at one of our establishments, you will enjoy personalized service and savor fresh-out-of-the oven breakfasts, lovingly prepared by our innkeepers, some of whom are accomplished professional chefs. Enjoy a hearty, mouthwatering start to your day before setting out to explore all that Rockport has to offer.

Our knowledgeable innkeepers are ready to help you plan your visit. Hike trails along our rugged coastline, sail, or whale watch. Relax at Front or Old Garden Beach, stroll through art galleries, museums, antique shops, boutiques and gardens. In the evening you might want to catch a lively local concert at the Back Beach bandstand, at one of our downtown restaurants or at the world-class Shalin Liu Performance Center.

The inspiration for this book comes from the hundreds of visitors from all over the globe who "enter our homes as strangers and leave as friends." We hope you enjoy learning about the history of our inns, the dedicated innkeepers who run them, and the signature recipes you have requested over the years. Even more, we hope you are inspired to start planning your next Rockport getaway!

So, grab a cup of coffee or "a proper cup of tea" and thumb through these pages for an enticing journey through our beloved Rockport and region commonly known as "the other cape," Cape Ann.

Fun Facts
*Rockport innkeepers are also an invaluable resource for helping you learn about and explore the treasures of the region that only locals would know. As you read through our cookbook, you'll discover **"fun facts"** of historical information, unique stories, events and places to visit.*

Acknowledgments

A huge thank you to the Rockport artists who contributed original art to our book! We cannot thank you enough for the part you and all the town's artists play to make Rockport a special place.

Cover Art and Design: David Arsenault
>The Art of David Arsenault
>www.artofdavid.com
>518-466-9093
>8 Dock Square, Rockport, MA
>Cover Painting: "Center of Attention"

Border Art: Lauri Kaihlanen
>Kaihlanen Galleries
>www.kaihlanengalleries.com
>978-546-9818
>61 Bearskin Neck, Rockport, MA

Compiled, Formatted and Edited by:
>Beth Cheney Roenker, Seafarer Inn

Publishing Consultant:
>Dan Duffy, Beech Tree Bed & Breakfast

Content Contributor:
>Helene Duffy, Beech Tree Bed & Breakfast

Recipe Consultant:
>Chef Sawsan Galal, Sally Webster Inn

Graphic Assistance:
>Tobey Shepherd, Linden Tree Inn
>Chris Roenker, Seafarer Inn

Proofreading and Additional Editing:
>Ellen Hale, Production Consultant
>Tracey Nestel, Lantana House B&B

Dedication

We dedicate this book to our cherished guests. It has been our pleasure over many years to make your visits to Rockport comfortable, relaxing and memorable. We have learned about your homes, families and travels, shared your joys and sorrows and made many, many friends. We love our jobs!

We hope you love Rockport as much as we do and that you enjoy our book!

The Inns of Rockport Cookbook

Contents

Breads & Muffins	9
Fruits & Smoothies	55
Cereals & Yogurts	67
Savory Breakfasts	77
Sweet Breakfasts	103
Appetizers	133
Soups	147
Main Dishes	163
Salads & Sides	191
Desserts	205
Jams, Jellies & Sauces	233
Odds & Ends	245
Index	257

Look for these symbols:
GF - Gluten Free   VG – Vegan

Breads And Muffins

The Tuck Inn

The Tuck Inn is one of the earliest traditional B&B's, operating in Rockport since 1947. This 1790 Colonial home touts 11 tastefully decorated rooms, that maintain the architectural details of the age combined with the modern conveniences of today. The renowned home-baked breakfast buffet, extensive gardens and hospitable atmosphere stressed by current owners Liz & Scott Wood over the last 28 years have made the Tuck Inn a local favorite.

Located in a quiet residential area of town, guests can enjoy most of the town on foot, as the village center with its dozens of shops, galleries and restaurants as well as two public beaches are all just a short stroll away. Additionally, our local train station servicing Salem and Boston is just a 15 minute walk too.

Rockport offers extraordinary coastal walks, the memorable Halibut State Park, and our world-class Shalin Liu Performance Center. Beyond our village, the fishing port of Gloucester is just 3 miles away. For history buffs, Salem is a half hour away and Boston is about an hour away by car or train. Rockport is ideally situated so near to everything North of Boston, including New Hampshire and Maine, that we strongly recommend guests use our town as their home base, but then come back to rest and relax in our quiet seaside village.

We warmly invite you to come stay with us in Rockport, Massachusetts.

The Tuck Inn B&B
17 High St., Rockport, Massachusetts 01966
978-546-7260
info@tuckinn.com
www.tuckinn.com

Blueberry Scones
Scott Wood, Tuck Inn

Ingredients:
2 cups flour
1/3 cup sugar
2 tsp baking powder
½ tsp baking soda
¼ tsp salt

3/4 cup lemon or vanilla yogurt
1 egg, lightly beaten
1/4 cup melted butter
1 tsp lemon peel
1 cup blueberries

Glaze:
½ cup confectioner's sugar
1 tbsp lemon juice
½ tsp lemon peel

Directions:
Preheat oven to 400. Combine dry ingredients. Combine butter, yogurt egg and lemon peel.

Stir moist ingredients into dry until just moistened. Fold in berries. Drop onto greased baking sheet.

Bake at 400 degrees for 15-18 minutes.

Spread glaze on scones while still warm. Yields 15-18 scones.

Squire Tarbox Inn Maine Blueberry-Nut Muffins

Scott Wood, Tuck Inn

Ingredients:

2 eggs	4 tsp baking powder
1 cup sugar	1 tsp salt
1 cup milk	1 cup blueberries
3 tbsp butter, melted & cooled	½ cup chopped walnuts
3 cups flour	Extra sugar for sprinkling

Directions:
Preheat oven to 375 and grease 16 large muffin cups.

Beat eggs and sugar until combined and thickened. Add milk and butter and beat well.

Set aside 2 tbsp of flour to mix with berries. Add the remaining flour, baking powder and salt to the batter and beat well to just mix.

Sprinkle the blueberries with the flour and add them to the batter with the walnuts, folding them in with a rubber spatula.

Divide the batter among the 16 muffin cups and sprinkle the tops with sugar. Bake for 25 minutes.

Corn Toasties or Muffins
Scott Wood, Tuck Inn

Ingredients:
1 ¼ cup flour	Pinch salt
¾ cup corn meal	1 cup milk
¼ cup sugar	¼ cup oil
2 tsp baking powder	1 egg, beaten

Directions:
Preheat oven to 400. Grease cast iron toasties pan or muffin tins.

Combine dry ingredients. Stir in milk, oil and egg, mixing just until dry ingredients are moistened.

Pour batter into prepared pan.

Bake 15-20 minutes or until light golden brown and wooden pick inserted in center comes out clean.

Bearskin Neck
Jutting into Sandy Bay, in the heart of downtown Rockport, is Bearskin Neck, named from a bear caught by the tide and killed in 1700. The Neck served as the commercial and shipbuilding center of Rockport for 160 years, and is now a collection of quaint homes, gift shops, galleries and restaurants. The first dock was built here in 1743. Sandy Bay Pier Company was organized in 1809. At the very end, you will see the site of Stone Fort and Sea Fencibles Barracks from the War of 1812.

Cranberry Coffee Cake

Scott Wood, Tuck Inn

Ingredients:
1 stick margarine
1 cup sugar
2 eggs
1 tsp baking powder
2 cups flour
1 tsp baking soda
½ tsp salt
1 7 oz can whole cranberry sauce
½ cup chopped nuts
½ pint sour cream
1 tsp almond flavoring

Topping:
¾ cup confectioner's sugar
2 tbsp warm water   ½ tsp almond flavoring

Directions:
Preheat oven to 350. Grease and flour tube pan.

Cream margarine with sugar. Add eggs and beat.

Combine and mix dry ingredients and add to above, alternately with sour cream and flavoring.

Place half of batter in pan; put half of cranberry sauce evenly on top. Add the rest of batter and then put rest of cranberry sauce around top. Sprinkle with nuts.

Bake in 350 degree oven for about 55 minutes. Remove from pan after 5 minutes.

Topping:
Mix ¾ cup confectioner's sugar, 2 tbsp warm water and ½ tsp almond flavoring. Spread on cooled cake and let it run on sides.

Blueberry Coffee Cake

Richard Nestel, Lantana House B&B

Ingredients:
Batter:

¾ cup sugar	2 tsp baking powder
4 tbsp butter	½ tsp salt
1 large egg	2 cups blueberries
½ cup milk	1 tsp vanilla extract
2 cups all-purpose flour	

Topping:

¾ cup sugar	½ tsp salt
¾ cup flour	5 tbsp butter
1 tsp cinnamon	

Directions:
Preheat oven to 375. Grease a 9x9 cake pan.

Cream the sugar and butter. Beat in the egg and vanilla.

Whisk together the dry ingredients. Add to the mixture alternatively with the milk. Fold in the blueberries. Pour into the pan.

In a bowl mix the topping ingredients. Cut in the butter till it is crumbly. Pour over the batter.

Bake for 45-50 minutes or until a cake tester comes out clean.

Tobey's Melt-In-Your-Mouth Legendary Scones
Tobey Shepherd, Linden Tree Inn

Ingredients:
1 ¾ cup flour
3 tbsp sugar
2 ½ tsp baking powder
½ tsp salt
1/3 cup butter (5 tbsp and 1 tsp)
1 egg, beaten
6-8 tbsp heavy cream, you want a slightly sticky not too stiff dough
½ cup or more dried fruits or mini semi-sweet chocolate chips, (I frequently use much more than half a cup)

Directions:
Preheat oven to 400. Sift dry ingredients together. Cut butter into dry ingredients. I use my Kitchen-Aid mixer to cut the butter in, but you can use 2 knives or a pastry blender.

Mix in dried fruits and/or nuts.

Beat egg with about ¼ cup or so of heavy cream. Pour egg/cream mixture into dry ingredients and mix. Continue adding in heavy cream 'till the scone mix is sticky.

Drop onto parchment or Silpat lined cookie sheet about size of a lime. You can make them bigger or smaller, just bake more or less. Bigger ones take longer to bake, and are more inclined to get too dark. (I use a cookie scoop size 20.)

Bake at 400 for 6 minutes. Then turn cookie sheet front to back so you can gauge if they need another 2-4 minutes. Ovens vary, so you might need to adjust the times to suit your oven. You want them to be light brown, not too dark, but baked, so they lightly spring back when you touch the top.

Tobey's Melt-In-Your-Mouth Legendary Scones
continued

Remove from oven, cool slightly before putting in basket or however you serve them. Don't pile too high when they are hot as they are very tender and will crumble or crush each other!

Serve with butter (if you dare) and jam! Devon clotted cream is nice if you can find it or if you are having a more formal tea.

Notes:
If doing the night before, you can make them so they are fairly moist but definitely not runny, especially if you use a cookie scoop to drop them. You do not want the dough to be too stiff or too dry, or you can just use a spoon to drop them.

I will make these the night before and put them on cookie sheets and place them in the 'fridge. Bake them right out of the 'fridge. The butter and cream get really cold and they become more flaky.

Melt-In-Your-Mouth Pumpkin Pecan Scones

Tobey Shepherd, Linden Tree Inn

Ingredients:
1 ¾ cup flour
3 tbsp sugar
2 ½ tsp baking powder
½ tsp salt
1/3 cup butter (5 tbsp and 1 tsp)
1 egg, beaten
6-8 tbsp heavy cream
1 ½ tsp cinnamon
1 tsp ginger
1 ½ tsp pumpkin pie spice
1 cup pecans, chopped
1/3 cup pumpkin butter

Directions:
Preheat oven to 400. Sift flour with sugar, baking powder and salt and spices. Cut butter with pastry blender or two knives method 'till crumbly. Alternatively, I have used my Kitchen Aid mixer with paddle attachment on the first slow setting to cut the butter in. Mix in pecans when butter is cut in.

In a separate bowl, hand whisk the egg, 2 tbsp of heavy cream and the pumpkin butter.

Add the egg mix to the dry mix, mix in and add in more cream 'till it forms a soft, slightly sticky dough in the mixer. If mixing by hand, I start with a wooden spoon and then use my hands to knead gently about 10 times.

Drop spoonsful of your desired size onto an ungreased cookie sheet. (I use my hands to make the size scone I like, but you can determine which method works best for you!) Bake about 10-14 minutes. Your oven time may vary.

Enjoy them warm from the oven. If you have any left over, you can warm them up in a 400 degree oven for about 5 minutes and they will freshen up nicely.

Sour Cream Coffee Cake

Tobey Shepherd, Linden Tree Inn

Ingredients:
3/4 cup shortening
3/4 cup sugar
2 cups flour
1/2 tsp salt
1 tsp baking powder
1 tsp baking soda
1 cup sour cream
2 eggs
1 tsp vanilla

Topping:
1/2 cup chopped walnuts
1/2 cup sugar
2 tsp cinnamon

Directions:
Preheat oven to 350. Cream shortening and sugar together. Add dry ingredients and mix. Add the rest of the ingredients. Pour into greased 9x9 inch pan and sprinkle with topping. Bake for 40-45 minutes or until done.

Notes:
If you double the recipe, use a Bundt pan and add time as it takes longer to bake. For the double recipe, I grease and flour the Bundt pan, put half of the topping in the bottom of the Bundt pan, then half the batter, then the other half of the topping, followed by the remaining batter. I love that layer of topping in between!

Fudgy Chocolate Gluten Free Vegan Muffins

Sawsan Galal, Sally Webster Inn

Ingredients:
2 cup cooked black beans
1 tbsp ground chia seeds or flax seeds + 3 tbsp water
1 cup oil
½ cup agave
1 tbsp vanilla
1 cup cocoa
½ cup gluten free flour
½ tsp baking soda
1 ½ cup shredded zucchini or applesauce, or cooked pears
Chopped nuts and raisins or Craisins (optional)

Directions:
Preheat oven to 350.

In a blender, mix black beans, agave, oil and chia seeds with water and vanilla. Blend until black beans are thoroughly pureed. Blend dry ingredients together. Fold in the two mixes and don't over beat.

Place in lined muffin tins and bake at 350 about 20-30 minutes. <u>Do not overbake</u>. Muffins should still be soft to the touch. For the muffins to hold their shape well, they must cool completely. They will have the consistency of a brownie.

Notes:
Do not overbake. Yields 3 dozen.

GF VG

Gluten Free Vegan Banana Muffins

Sawsan Galal, Sally Webster Inn

Ingredients:
3 large bananas, mashed
¾ cup vegetable oil
½ cup soy milk or any other kind of milk
1 tbsp milled chia or flax seeds
1 tsp vanilla extract
3-4 drops banana extract oil (optional)
3 tbsp water
2 cups gluten free flour
1 tsp baking powder
½ tsp baking soda
¼ tsp salt
¾ cup sugar
½ cup ground pecans or any other nuts

Directions:
Preheat oven to 375.

Mix wet ingredients together. Mix dry ingredients separately. Place both mixes in a larger bowl and fold just until well mixed. Do not over-mix.

Scoop into paper lined muffin tins.

Bake at 375 for about 10 minutes. Do not over bake.

Notes:
Do not overbake. Makes 18 muffins.

GF VG

Cranberry Apple Walnut Bread

Scott Wood, Tuck Inn

Ingredients:

2 cups apples, peeled and chopped (bite size)
½ cup sugar
2 tbsp oil
1 egg
1 cup flour + ½ cup wheat flour
1½ tsp baking powder
½ tsp baking soda
1 tsp cinnamon
1 cup fresh cranberries
½ cup walnuts
(Add 1/8 to 1/4 cup milk if too dry.)

Directions:
Preheat oven to 350.

Combine apples, sugar, oil and egg; mix together and then add all dry ingredients.

Add cranberries and walnuts and mix gently.

Spread batter into greased loaf pan.

Bake at 350 for 1 hour.

Apple Cider Baked Doughnuts with Maple Glaze

Sawsan Galal, Sally Webster Inn

Ingredients:

Doughnuts:

1/3 cup vegetable oil	1 ½ tsp vanilla
3 large eggs	1 tsp cinnamon
1 ¼ cups granulated sugar	1 tsp salt
1 cup unsweetened applesauce	1 ½ tsp baking powder
¼ cup boiled apple cider (or 6 tbsp applesauce)	2 cups + 2 tbsp flour (or GF flour or wheat flour)

Coating:
2 tbsp cinnamon-sugar

Glaze:

1 ½ cups confectioner's sugar	Pinch of salt
2 tbsp maple syrup	2 tsp milk or 1 tbsp heavy cream
¾ tsp maple flavor (optional)	

Directions:

Preheat oven to 350. Lightly grease a standard doughnut pan.

Beat together the oil, eggs, sugar, applesauce, boiled cider, vanilla, cinnamon, salt and baking powder until smooth. Add the flour, stirring just until smooth. Fill the wells of the doughnut pans nearly to the rim.

Bake for 15-18 minutes or until a cake tester inserted into the center of one comes out clean. Remove the doughnuts from the oven and loosen the edges. After about 5 minutes, transfer them to a rack. While the doughnuts are still warm, but no longer fragile, gently shake them 1 or 2 at a time, in a bag with the cinnamon-sugar.

Mix together the glaze and spread on the doughnuts. Return to the rack and let cool.

Fruit and Nut Bread
Scott Wood, Tuck Inn

Ingredients:

2 cups chopped dates (or apricots or raisins or dried cranberries)
1 cup chopped pecans (or walnuts)
1 tsp baking soda
2 cups flour

1 cup boiling water
1 tsp vanilla
1 egg
¼ tsp salt
1 stick butter
¾ cup packed brown sugar

Directions:
Preheat oven to 350. Grease and flour 2 8x4 inch loaf pans.

Stir baking soda and salt into boiling water; pour water over fruit and let set for ten minutes.

Meanwhile, cream butter, brown sugar and vanilla.

Beat in egg.

Add fruit mixture and stir well; beat in flour. Add nuts.

Pour into greased loaf pans and bake at 350 until done, approximately 45 minutes.

Let cool and sprinkle with confectioner's sugar.

Notes:
Keeps well in the 'fridge.

Lemon Bread

Scott Wood, Tuck Inn

Ingredients:
1½ cups flour	2 eggs
1 tsp baking powder	½ cup shortening
½ tsp salt	½ cup milk
1 cup sugar	grated rind of 1 lemon

Glaze:
¾ cup confectioner's sugar
juice of one lemon

Directions:
Preheat oven to 350. Cream shortening and sugar.

Add eggs and beat well.

Sift dry ingredients and add to creamed mixture alternately with milk.

Fold in lemon rind.

Bake at 350 for 30-40 minutes.

Pierce top of cake with fork tines several times and pour glaze over cake as soon as it is removed from oven so that the glaze pours into the cake.

Lemon Nut Bread

Tobey Shepherd by way of Penny Olson, Linden Tree Inn

Ingredients:
½ cup margarine or butter
2 eggs
1 cup sugar
1 ½ cups sifted flour
1 ½ tsp baking powder
½ tsp salt
½ cup milk
½ cup chopped nuts
Grated rind of 1 lemon

After bread is baked you need:
1/3 cup sugar
The juice of one lemon

Directions:
Preheat oven to 350.

Cream together the margarine (or butter), eggs, and sugar. Sift together and add the flour, baking powder and salt. Add milk, nuts and lemon rind.

Bake at 350, in greased loaf pan, for one hour.

Mix together the juice of 1 lemon and 1/3 cup sugar. While bread is still hot, insert a skewer into bread in several places and pour the sugar mixture over the bread into the holes.

Notes:
Penny notes, "for easier grating, freeze the lemon rind."

This is an heirloom Linden Tree recipe, from the archives of an old newsletter.

Maple-Walnut Scones

Scott Wood, Tuck Inn

Ingredients:

3 ½ cups flour	2/3 cup vegetable shortening or butter
1 cup finely chopped walnuts	1 cup milk
4 tsp baking powder	½ cup maple syrup, separated
1 tsp salt	½ tsp maple flavoring
Extra flour (for sprinkling)	

Directions:
Preheat oven to 425. Grease a large baking sheet.

In a large bowl, combine flour, chopped walnuts, baking powder and salt.

With pastry blender or two knives, cut in shortening until mixture resembles coarse crumbs.

Add the milk, 1/3 cup of the maple syrup and the maple flavoring and mix lightly with a fork until the mixture clings together and forms a soft dough.

Turn the dough out onto a lightly floured surface and knead it gently 5 or 6 times.

Divide the dough in half. With a lightly floured rolling pin, roll one half into a 7-inch round. Cut it into 8 wedges. Repeat with the remaining half.

Place the scones on a baking sheet and use a fork to pierce the tops.

Brush them with the remaining maple syrup.

Bake scones for 15 to 18 minutes until golden. Serve warm

Mary Richardson's Irish Bread
Scott Wood, Tuck Inn

Ingredients:
1 cup whole-wheat flour
1 cup white flour
¼ tsp salt
½ tsp cream of tartar

1 cup milk (about)
2 oz or 4 tbsp butter or margarine
½ tsp baking soda

Directions:
Preheat oven to 350. Mix dry ingredients together. Cut in butter or margarine till crumbly.

Add as much milk as necessary to make dough that is easy to handle but not sticky.

Knead by hand on a floured board until smooth.

Flatten into a circle about 1 ½ inches thick.

Cut an X across the surface and transfer dough to lightly greased cookie sheet.

Bake in preheated oven at 350 for 50 minutes

Oatmeal Pecan Muffins

Scott Wood, Tuck Inn

Ingredients:
1 1/3 cups uncooked quick oats
1 ¼ cups flour
½ cup sugar
1 tbsp baking powder
½ tsp salt
1/3 cup cold butter
1 cup half & half
1 egg, lightly beaten
½ cup chopped pecans

Directions:
Preheat oven to 400.

Combine oats, flour, sugar, baking powder and salt in large bowl; cut in butter with pastry blender or fork until mixture resembles coarse crumbs.

Stir in half & half and egg just until moistened.

Gently stir in pecans.

Spoon batter evenly into 12 paper-lined or greased muffin cups.

Bake at 400 for 17-20 minutes

Pumpkin Bread
Scott Wood, Tuck Inn

Ingredients:
3 cups sugar
1 cup of oil
4 eggs
1 can of Pumpkin (1 ¾ cup)
3 ½ cups flour
2 tsp salt

1 tsp baking powder
1 tsp cinnamon
2 tsp baking soda
1 tsp allspice
½ tsp cloves
2/3 cup water

Directions:
Preheat oven to 350.

Add sugar to oil, then add eggs one at a time.
Add pumpkin.

Sift together remaining ingredients.

Mix dry ingredients into pumpkin mixture alternately with 2/3 cup water.

Bake for one hour in 3 8x4 loaf pans and one 5x3 pan that have been greased and floured.

Rhubarb Streusel Bread
Scott Wood, Tuck Inn

Bread Ingredients:
1 cup sugar
1/2 cup butter, softened
1/3 cup orange juice
2 eggs
2 cups all-purpose flour

1 tsp baking powder
1/4 tsp baking soda
1/4 tsp salt
1 ½ cups (1/4-inch) sliced fresh rhubarb

Streusel Ingredients:
2 tbsp sugar
2 tbsp packed brown sugar
1 tbsp all-purpose flour

1 tbsp melted butter
1 ½ tsp cinnamon

Directions:
Preheat oven to 350. Combine sugar and butter in large bowl and beat until creamy. Add orange juice and eggs and continue to beat on low until just mixed (mixture will look slightly curdled).

Stir in flour, baking powder, soda and salt by hand just until moistened. Gently stir in rhubarb (batter will be thick). <u>Reserve 1½ cups batter.</u> Pour remaining batter into greased & floured 8x4 loaf pan.

Combine all streusel ingredients in small bowl; stir until mixture resembles coarse crumbs.

Sprinkle half of streusel over batter in pan; gently press into the batter. Spread reserved batter into pan; top with remaining streusel (press into batter).

Bake at 350 for 65-70 minutes. A great bake ahead-bread as flavor increases with time.

Popovers

Lynne Norris, Pleasant Street Inn

These are a family favorite!

Ingredients:
3 eggs
1 1/3 cup milk
1 cup flour
1 tsp salt
1 tbsp melted butter

Directions:
Preheat oven to 450. Mix all the ingredients for about 15 seconds in a blender.

Spray a popover pan with non-stick spray (such as Pam.) Use plenty. Pour mixture into greased pan.

Bake at 450 for 20 minutes, then turn oven down to 350 and continue baking for 18 minutes.

Remove from oven and pierce the top of each popover with a sharp knife.

Millbrook Meadow
Rockport has a four-acre park right across the street from Front Beach. Nearly half of it is a Mill Pond and a pristine wonderland of aquatic plants, complete with turtles, eels, ducks, otters, beavers and a few fish. You can skate on our Pond in wintertime. You can play or walk or simply sit and enjoy our parkland in Millbrook Meadow 'most any time of the year. During the summer, we have fairs and music festivals in the Meadow.

Sour Cream Bundt Coffee Cake

Richard Nestel, Lantana House B&B

Ingredients:
Cake:
2 cups flour
1 tsp baking powder
1 tsp baking soda
1 cup sugar
¼ lb (1 stick) butter
1 tsp vanilla extract
2 eggs beaten
1 cup sour cream

Filling/Topping:
½ cup brown sugar
1 tsp cinnamon
½ cup chopped pecans

Directions:
Preheat oven to 350. Grease and flour a Bundt pan.

Cream the butter and sugar. Add the eggs and vanilla.

Add the dry ingredients alternatively with the sour cream.

Pour half the batter into the pan. Cover with half the topping. Pour in remaining batter. Cover with the remaining topping.

Bake for 40 minutes.

Anadama Bread

Chris Roenker, Seafarer Inn

Anadama Bread is a sweet, brown molasses bread that tastes like old fashioned beach vacations. It is also a Cape Ann invention. There are as many recipes as there are stories of the origin of Anadama Bread. Here are two stories and my recipe.

The story goes that there was a fisherman, whose wife, Anna, prepared nothing for him to eat but a bowl of cornmeal and molasses. One day, he added yeast and flour to his daily gruel in order to make bread – just something different! As he went about his chore he grumbled, "Anna, damn her!"

A more endearing version of the story tells of a sea captain whose wife, Anna, was quite a good baker and known for her cornmeal and molasses bread. This story tells us that after she died, on her gravestone he put, "Anna was a lovely bride, but Anna, damn her, up and died."

Ingredients:
½ cup coarse cornmeal
2 ¼ cup boiling water
1 tsp salt
4 tbsp butter
1 cup molasses
2 ¼ tsp dried yeast
¼ cup warm water
5 cup unbleached flour

Directions:
Stir the cornmeal slowly into the boiling water and steam over a double boiler for an hour.* (You can do this step one day ahead of time.)

Add the butter, molasses and salt and let cool.

In the meantime, dissolve the yeast in ¼ cup warm water.

Anadama Bread continued

When the cornmeal mixture is lukewarm, add the dissolved yeast.

Add the flour and knead for 10 minutes.

Put dough into a greased bowl and cover with a damp cloth for 1 ½ hours.

Grease two bread pans and put ½ the dough in each and let rise for another hour (uncovered.)

Bake at 350 for 40 minutes.   Let stand for 10 minutes.

Notes:
No need for butter, this bread is moist and delicious.

We like it with yogurt, peanut butter or applesauce on top.

Anadama Bread makes a great French Toast!!

*Shortcut: if you can't find coarse cornmeal, you can use standard corn meal. If you do, you will save time. It steams in 5 minutes.

Rich Biscuits
Scott Wood, Tuck Inn

Ingredients:
4 cups all-purpose flour
6 tbsp butter or marg.
4 tbsp other shortening
½ tsp salt
1 tbsp sugar

8 tsp baking powder
1 ½ tsp cream of tartar
2 eggs
1 cup milk

Directions:
Sift dry ingredients together. Mix or cut in shortening until consistency of corn meal.

Beat eggs and combine with milk. Make well in center of dry ingredients, add egg-milk mixture. Stir just until blended with spatula. Do not beat.

Turn out on slightly floured board, knead lightly for a few minutes.

Pat out to about ¾ inch thickness and cut with 1 ½ inch glass. Place close together on slightly greased baking sheet, let stand about 10 minutes. Meanwhile, preheat the oven to 450.

Bake at 450 for 5 minutes. Lower heat to 425 and bake 10 minutes or until nice and brown.

Makes 24 biscuits.

Sweet Muffins
Scott Wood, Tuck Inn

Ingredients:
1 egg
½ cup milk
¼ cup oil
½ tsp salt

1 ½ cup flour
½ cup sugar
2 tsp baking powder

Directions:
Preheat oven to 400. Grease muffin tins.

Beat egg.

Stir in milk and oil.

Add other ingredients and mix until moistened.

Bake for 20-25 minutes.

Notes:
Add fruit or nuts if desired. Makes 10-12 muffins

Thacher Island, Twin Lights
Thacher Island was sighted by Samuel de Champlain in 1605, by Captain John Smith in 1614 and by how many more before that, nobody knows. The name comes from a shipwreck described as "pathetic" by historians. A small boat out of Ipswich, bound for Marblehead, was caught in the Great Storm of August, 1635 and was dashed to pieces on the rocks of the Island. Of the twenty-three passengers and crew, only Anthony Thacher and his wife survived, watching helplessly as their children and friends were swept away. The island is home to the only twin lighthouses in America.

Wisconsin Apple Bread

Scott Wood, Tuck Inn

Ingredients:
1 stick butter
1 cup sugar
1 egg, beaten
2 cups flour
1 tsp baking soda
½ tsp salt
¼ tsp cinnamon
½ cup milk
1 ½ to 2 cups apples, pared, sliced thin
¼ cup chopped nuts (optional)

Directions:
Preheat oven to 350. Cream butter; add sugar and egg and beat well.

Sift dry ingredients and add to butter mixture alternately with milk.

Fold in apples and nuts.

Pour batter into well-greased and floured 9x5x3-inch pan. Sprinkle with sugar.

Bake at 350 for 50-60 minutes.

Rhubarb Streusel Muffins

Stephanie Smith, Changing Tides Bed & Breakfast

Ingredients:

½ cup butter or margarine, softened
1 cup brown sugar, packed
½ cup granulated sugar
1 egg
2 cups all-purpose flour
1 tsp baking powder
½ tsp baking soda
1/8 tsp salt
1 cup sour cream
3 cups fresh OR frozen rhubarb, chopped into 1" pieces*

Topping:

¼ cup pecans, chopped
¼ cup brown sugar, packed
½ tsp cinnamon
1 tbsp cold butter or margarine
1 tbsp all-purpose flour

Directions:
Preheat oven to 350. In a mixing bowl, cream butter and sugars. Add egg, beat well. Combine the flour, baking powder, baking soda and salt. Add to the creamed mixture alternately with the sour cream. Fold in the rhubarb.
Fill paper-lined or greased muffins tins 3/4 full.

For the topping:
In a small bowl, combine the pecans, brown sugar, flour and cinnamon. Cut in butter until crumbly.
Sprinkle over muffin batter in muffin tins.

Bake muffins at 350 for 22 -25 minutes or until a toothpick inserted in the center comes out clean.
Cool for 5 minutes before removing from pan.

Notes:
Makes about 1 - 1 1/2 dozen muffins.
*If you use *frozen* rhubarb, use it when the rhubarb is only *partially thawed* and discard any extra liquid.

Rhubarb Streusel Coffee Cake

Stephanie Smith, Changing Tides Bed & Breakfast

Ingredients:
Cake:
1 stick butter, softened, plus a bit more for the pan
1 cup brown sugar
2 eggs
1 tsp vanilla extract
2 cups flour
1 tsp baking soda
1 tsp baking powder
1 tsp salt
3/4 cup yogurt
¼ cup half & half
4 large stalks rhubarb, in ½ inch slices
1 tbsp sugar

Streusel:
1 cup plus 2 tbsp all-purpose flour
1/3 cup brown sugar
½ tsp cinnamon
½ tsp salt
¾ stick (6 tbsp) butter, softened but cool

Directions:
For the streusel:
Combine the flour, sugar, cinnamon and salt in a medium bowl, or the bowl of a stand mixer. Add the butter, and work with your fingers or paddle on low until the mixture begins to clump together. Set aside at room temperature.

For the cake:
Position a rack in the center of the oven and preheat to 350. Grease a 9x9x2-inch square pan generously with butter.

In the bowl of a stand mixer fitted with the paddle (or a bowl with a wooden spoon if you are strong) cream the butter and sugar together on medium until light and fluffy, 3 – 4 minutes, scraping down the sides of the bowl as necessary.

Rhubarb Streusel Coffee Cake continued

Add the eggs one at a time, beating until combined after each, then stir in the vanilla.

While the wets are doing their thing, sift the dries into a medium bowl.

Toss the rhubarb with the tbsp of sugar and set aside.

Stir together the yogurt and half & half.

With the mixer on low, alternate adding the dries and the dairy in three parts, beginning and ending with the dries and mixing until just combined after each addition. Give the batter a fold with a rubber spatula to make sure it is homogenous.

Spread a little more than half the batter in the bottom of the pan.

Sprinkle the rhubarb evenly over the top.

Cover with the rest of the batter, and sprinkle with the streusel, squeezing into almond sized clumps if necessary.

Bake for 50-60 minutes until it is golden brown, beginning to pull away from the sides, springs back to the touch, and passes the toothpick test.

Let cool for about 1 hour. Cut into 16 squares.

Makes one 9x9 coffeecake, sixteen 2-inch square pieces

Gluten Free Pumpkin Spice Coffee Cake with Cream Cheese Frosting

Debbie Benn, Seven South Street Inn

Ingredients:

- 4 eggs
- 1 cup sugar
- ¼ cup brown sugar
- 1 cup oil
- 1 tsp vanilla
- 2 cups sifted gluten free flour (I use Bob's Red Mill 1 to 1)
- 1 15 oz can pumpkin puree
- 2 tsp baking powder
- 1 tsp baking soda
- 2 tsp ground cinnamon
- 1 tsp ground nutmeg
- ¼ tsp ground clove
- ½ tsp salt

Directions:

Preheat oven to 350. Prepare a 9x13 baking dish with cooking spray.

Using an electric mixer at medium speed, combine the eggs, sugar, oil, vanilla and pumpkin until light and fluffy.

Sift together the flour, baking powder, baking soda, salt and spices.

Add the dry ingredients to the pumpkin mixture and mix at low speed until thoroughly mixed.

Spread the batter in prepared baking dish. Bake for 35-40 minutes or until a tooth pick inserted in the center comes out clean.

GF

Gluten Free Pumpkin Spice Coffee Cake with Cream Cheese Frosting continued

To make the Icing:
1 package (brick) of cream cheese
2-3 cups sifted confectioner's sugar
1 stick of butter, room temperature
1 tsp vanilla, GF

Combine the cream cheese and butter in a medium bowl with an electric mixer until smooth.

Add the sugar and vanilla and mix at low speed until smooth.

Cool cake completely and spread on the icing.

GF

Rockport Granite
By the beginning of the 19th century, the first granite quarries were developed and, by the 1830s, Rockport granite was being shipped to cities and towns throughout the east coast of the United States. As the demand for its high-grade granite grew during the Industrial Revolution, the quarries of Rockport became a major source of the stone. A distinctive form of sloop was even developed to transport the granite to parts far and wide until the second decade of the 20th century. For many years, there was a large number of residents of Scandinavian descent, dating from the days when Finnish and Swedish immigrants with stone-working expertise made up a large part of the workforce at the quarries.

No Yeast Cinnamon Rolls

Debbie Benn, Seven South Street Inn

This recipe is truly a guest favorite. This was given to me by my sister-in-law, Laurie Benn.

Ingredients:
Filling:
4 tbsp butter, room temp
1 cup packed brown sugar
2 tbsp ground cinnamon

Dough:
2 cups bread flour + more for rolling
2 tbsp sugar
3 tsp baking powder
1/4 tsp salt
3 tbsp butter, at room temperature
3/4 cup milk
1 large egg, beaten

Cream Cheese Frosting:
2 oz cream cheese, room temp
2/3 cup powdered sugar
3 tbsp milk

Directions:
Preheat the oven to 400. Spray muffin tin with nonstick spray.

Prepare the filling: In a small bowl, combine the ingredients with a fork until crumbly.

Prepare the dough: In a large bowl, whisk together the flour, sugar, baking powder and salt. Using a pastry blender or two knives work the butter into the dry ingredients. Add the milk and egg, stir to combine.

Roll the dough out on a floured surface into a roughly shaped large rectangle (1/4 inch thick). Sprinkle the filling evenly over the surface of the dough, leaving a ½ border at the top of long side.

No Yeast Cinnamon Rolls continued

Carefully roll up the rectangle, (the dough will be soft so flour hands as needed to prevent the dough from sticking.)

Cut the roll into 12 even pieces. Carefully place the rolls in prepared muffin tins.

Bake for 20-25 minutes.

While the rolls are baking, prepare the frosting:

Combine the cream cheese, powdered sugar and milk in a medium bowl. Use an electric mixer to combine.

Spread or drizzle the frosting on top of warm rolls. Serve warm.

The James Babson Cooperage Shop
The cooperage shop, a small one-story brick structure filled with early American tools and furniture, is located midway between Gloucester and Rockport. Built in 1658, it is considered the oldest building and the first "factory" on Cape Ann. Originally known as the James Babson Farm, James and his wife Elinor Hill settled on these 32 acres above "the Mill". At this stone shop, James made barrels that were taken to Good Harbor Beach to be filled with fish and shipped to England, the West Indies and other places around the world.

Pumpkin Spice Muffins or Coffee Cake
Debbie Benn, Seven South Street Inn

Ingredients:
¾ cup canned pumpkin
1 cup avocado oil
1 cup brown sugar, packed
2 cups flour
2 tsp baking powder
1 tsp baking soda
¼ tsp salt
1/8 tsp ground clove

¼ tsp ground allspice
½ tsp cinnamon
½ tsp ground nutmeg
2 eggs
1/3 cup slivered almonds or chopped pecans (optional)
¼ cup brown sugar to use as topping (optional)

Directions:
Preheat the oven to 350. Prepare 12-16 muffin tins or an 8x11 inch baking dish with cooking spray.

Blend the pumpkin, oil and sugar with an electric mixer at medium speed. Beat the eggs one at a time into the pumpkin mixture.

Sift together the dry ingredients including the spices. Gradually add this to the pumpkin mix, beating after each addition. Add the nuts at this time if using.

Place the mixture into 12-16 muffin tins using an ice cream scoop or pour into an 8X11 sprayed casserole dish and top with brown sugar if using.

Bake for 20-25 minutes for muffins or 25-30 minutes for coffee cake. Done when a tooth pick is inserted into the center and it comes out clean.

French Apple Cake

Jennifer Segal submitted by Debbie Benn, Seven South Street Inn

Ingredients:
1 cup flour, spooned into measuring cup and leveled-off
1 tsp baking powder
1 stick room temperature butter
2/3 cup sugar
2 large eggs
1 tsp vanilla extract
2-3 tbsp dark rum like Meyers
2 baking apples, I like Honeycrisp
Confectioner's sugar

Directions:
Preheat oven to 350. Line a 9-inch springform pan with parchment paper and then spray sides and corners with nonstick cooking spray.

In a small bowl, whisk together the flour, baking powder and salt. Using a handheld mixer, cream the butter and sugar until light and fluffy; about 3 minutes. Add the eggs, one at a time, beating well and scraping down the sides of the bowl after each addition. Beat in vanilla and rum. Don't worry if the batter looks grainy.

Add the flour mixture and mix on low speed until just combined. Using a rubber spatula, fold in the chopped apples.

Pour the batter into the prepared pan. Bake 30-40 minutes or until the cake is lightly golden and a toothpick inserted in the center comes out clean. Allow the cake to cool until just warm. Loosen the springform pan and remove sides. Dust the top with confectioner's sugar.

Notes:
Our Inn uses this sweetbread as one of our breakfast courses. You can also use as a dessert served with lightly sweetened whipped cream or vanilla ice cream.

Gluten Free French Apple Cake

Debbie Benn, Seven South Street Inn

Ingredients:

1 cup GF flour, spooned into measuring cup and leveled-off (I use Bob's Red Mill 1 to 1)
1 tsp baking powder
½ tsp baking soda
1 stick room temperature butter
2/3 cup sugar
3 eggs
1 tsp vanilla extract
2 tbsp dark rum like Meyers
2 baking apples, I like Honeycrisp
Confectioner's sugar

Directions:
Preheat oven to 350. Line a 9-inch springform pan with parchment paper and then spray sides and corners with nonstick cooking spray.

In a small bowl, whisk together the flour, baking powder, baking soda and salt. Using a handheld mixer, cream the butter and sugar until light and fluffy; about 3 minutes. Add the eggs, one at a time, beating well and scraping down the sides of the bowl after each addition. Beat in vanilla and rum. Don't worry if the batter looks grainy.

Add the flour mixture and mix on low speed until just combined. Using a rubber spatula, fold in the chopped apples.

Pour the batter into the prepared pan. Bake 40-55 minutes or until the cake is lightly golden and a toothpick inserted in the center comes out clean. Allow the cake to cool until just warm. Loosen the springform pan and remove sides. Dust the top with confectioner's sugar.

Notes:
I adapted this version from Jennifer's to accommodate gluten free flour. I can serve this cake and no-one knows it is gluten free.
GF

Gluten Free Blueberry Oatmeal Breakfast Bread
Debbie Benn, Seven South Street Inn

This will be the easiest breakfast bread you have ever made and tastes so good. It was given to me by my good friend, Lynne Morrill.

Ingredients:
1 ¼ cups of gluten free flour
¾ cup gluten free oats
½ cup sugar
2 tsp baking powder
¼ tsp salt
¾ cup milk
¼ cup vegetable oil
2 eggs
1 cup frozen wild blueberries
½ cup chopped walnuts or pecans

Directions:
Preheat oven to 400. Grease an 8-inch round spring form pan and line the bottom with parchment paper and spray the entire pan using cooking spray.

Combine the flour, oats, sugar, baking powder, and salt in a mixing bowl. Stir to combine.

In a large 3-4 cup measuring cup, add the milk, oil and then the eggs. Whisk. Add this mixture to the flour mixture. Stir until the batter is just combined (it will be lumpy.)
Gently fold in the blueberries and nuts (if using.)

Pour the batter into the prepared baking pan. Bake for 25-30 minutes or until the top is golden brown and a tooth pick inserted in the center comes out clean.
Remove the pan from the oven and let stand a few minutes before removing the spring sides. Cool for 5-10 minutes before cutting.

Serve warm, dusted with powder sugar.
GF

My Mom's Buttermilk Cornbread

Debbie Benn, Seven South Street Inn

This recipe was given to me by my Mom, Dottie P. when I first started operating the Inn in February 2000! It's still a favorite.

Ingredients:
1 stick butter, melted
½ cup sugar
¼ cup honey
2 eggs, room temperature
1 cup buttermilk, room temperature (this recipe uses buttermilk only)

1 cup flour
1 cup cornmeal
½ tsp baking soda
1 15 oz size can whole kernel corn, drained very well
1 tbsp sugar (optional)

Directions:
Preheat oven to 375. Lightly butter an 8x8 or 9x9 inch glass baking pan, set aside.

In a large mixing bowl, combine the melted butter, sugar and honey. Wisk in the eggs one at a time, beating until the mixture is smooth. Add the buttermilk and mix.

In a medium mixing bowl whisk together the flour, cornmeal, salt and baking soda. Gradually add the dry ingredients to the wet, stirring with a spatula until only a few lumps remain. Add the corn and mix.

Pour the batter into the prepared pan, smooth the top, (if you prefer a sweeter bread, sprinkle top with 1 Tbsp of sugar).

Bake for 25-35 minutes or until the top is golden brown and a cake tester inserted in the middle comes out clean.

Allow the bread to cool slightly before serving warm.

Fool Proof (and Easy) Banana Bread
Rosemarie Cerundolo, Periwinkle Cottage

This recipe is delicious and if you have leftovers, make French toast!

Ingredients:
½ cup Crisco
2 cups flour
1 cup sugar
½ tsp salt
2 eggs, beaten, divided
1 tsp baking soda
1 tsp baking powder
3 large or 5 small ripe bananas
Walnuts (optional)

Directions:
Preheat oven to 350. Grease loaf pan.

Cream shortening and sugar well. Add beaten eggs one at a time.

Add flour, salt, baking soda and powder.

Mash bananas and add in banana pulp and mix well. If using nuts, sprinkle on top.

Pour into pan and bake 1 hour.

The Most Versatile Coffee Cake (or Muffin Mix) EVER

Debbie Benn, Seven South Street Inn

Ingredients:
1 stick of butter, softened
1 cup sugar
2 eggs
1 ¼ cups sour cream
1 tsp vanilla extract
2 cups flour
2 tsp baking powder
1 tsp baking soda
¼ tsp salt
Dash of nutmeg

Directions:
Preheat oven to 350. With an electric mixer, cream together butter and sugar. Beat in eggs, then sour cream and vanilla.

In a separate bowl or in a sifter, sift together flour, baking powder and baking soda, salt and nutmeg.

Slowly mix flour mixture into batter (do not over-mix). Batter will be thick.

Pour batter into a well-buttered 9x11 baking dish (or muffin tins) top with sugar, cinnamon sugar or nuts.

Bake at 350 for 35 to 45 minutes or until a toothpick inserted in the center comes out clean. Remove from oven and cool before cutting. Yields 1 large coffee cake or 16-18 muffins

Notes:
I used to make all different kinds of coffee cakes and muffins with a different recipe for each until I discovered that, using this one basic mix, I could turn the batter into whatever kind of muffins or coffee cake desired. Here are some of the variations that I use. Possibilities are endless!

The Most Versatile Coffee Cake (or Muffin Mix)
EVER continued

- Blueberry, add about one cup fresh or frozen to the batter.
- Chocolate chips, minis work well when using for breakfast.
- Chocolate chip and chopped walnuts (Oh so good!)
- Slivered Almonds and 1 tsp almond extract instead of the vanilla, top with sliced almonds and powdered sugar.
- 1 apple and a half cup frozen cranberries to batter, add ½ cup chopped nuts even better.
- Top batter with slices of peeled pear, arranged all over the top and drizzle with maple syrup.
- This one is oh so yummy. Mix canned crushed pineapple, well drained into some cream cheese. Sweeten with sugar to taste. After the batter has been put in the pan, dollop the mixture all over the batter and swirl with a knife. Top with white sugar.
- Cream cheese mixed with your favorite jam, like raspberry, strawberry, mixed berry… the list is endless. Same as above, dollop and swirl with a knife.
- Mix batter with brown sugar instead of white and top batter with washed and dried red or green seedless grapes. Top with a thin layer of brown sugar. This is so good. When the grapes are cooked, they almost taste like sweet wine without the alcohol.

Be creative and *enjoy!*

Motif # 1

The iconic red shack seen from T-Wharf and located on Bradley Wharf in Rockport Harbor, is Motif #1. The Motif is a former fishing shack known as "the most often-painted building in America." The current building is actually a replica of the original. The original structure was built in 1840 and destroyed in the Blizzard of 1978, and after a vote by the townspeople, the exact reproduction was constructed that same year.

In the 1800's, Rockport was becoming home to a colony of artists as well as a settlement of fishermen. In addition to its primary purpose as storage for fishing equipment, the shack became a favorite subject of painters who loved the location and the unique quality of light in Rockport Harbor. Painter Lester Hornby (1882–1956) is believed to be the first to call the shack Motif #1, and the name achieved general acceptance. The shack has become a symbol of, not only Rockport, but of the New England coast.

The Inns of Rockport Cookbook

Fruits & Smoothies

Seven South Street Inn

The "breakfast" in Bed and Breakfast is Debbie and Nick Benn's favorite thing about being innkeepers. We love starting our day with good cooking and good conversation. Our guests love us for it. Visitors to the Inn have filled guestbook after guestbook with accolades for our beautiful and interesting rooms, but the artful, creative, almost sinful four-course breakfast dining is the hallmark of Seven South Street Inn.

A four-course breakfast is served in the dining room each morning at 8 & 9. The meal begins with an artfully arranged fresh fruit plate. Course two is homemade sweet bread such as pumpkin spice coffee cake. That is followed by a fluted glass of blended frozen fruits, juice and yogurt and then a hot breakfast entrée of the day which alternates daily between sweet and savory. Some of the guests' favorite dishes from the long list of menu items include Eggs Benedict, Peaches and Cream Belgian Waffles and thick Pineapple Stuffed French Toast, topped with warm blueberry compote.

Each room is unique in color and décor. We have enjoyed renovating and decorating each guest room and the Inn's public spaces. Great time and care have gone into each thoughtfully appointed guest room. After all, the Seven South Street Inn is not only our business but also our home. For a full list of amenities, rates and discounts and also to view our guests' rooms visit our website at www.sevensouthstreetinn.com.

Seven South Street Inn
7 South St., Rockport, Massachusetts 01966
978-546-6708
theinn@sevensouth.net
www.sevensouthstreetinn.com

Roasted Mascarpone Peaches

Debbie Benn, Seven South Street Inn

A refreshing breakfast course or can be used as a dessert.

Ingredients:
4 large, ripe peaches
8 oz mascarpone cheese
2 tbsp vanilla sugar or light brown sugar
Mint garnish

Directions:
Preheat oven to 400.

Cut peaches in half, remove pits and place cut-side up in a roasting pan.

Sprinkle the tops with the vanilla sugar or light brown sugar and bake for 20-30 minutes or until soft.

Change oven to broil and put under the open flame for a couple of minutes, watching constantly so they don't burn.

Mix the mascarpone with 2 tbsp of vanilla sugar. Dollop a spoonful on top of each peach and garnish with mint.

Serve warm.

GF

Poached Pears

Sawsan Galal, Sally Webster Inn

Ingredients:
½ tbsp cardamom pods
2 cups dry white wine
¾ cup sugar
1 whole cinnamon stick
1 ½ tbsp fresh lemon juice
Pinch of kosher salt
4 firm pears, peeled, stems intact
1 6 oz container crème fraiche or your favorite ice cream

Directions:
Gently crush cardamom with a rolling pin or the bottom of a skillet to slightly crack open pods without releasing seeds.

Combine cardamom, wine, sugar, lemon juice, cinnamon stick and salt in a medium saucepan over medium heat, stirring until sugar dissolves. Bring to a simmer. Add pears; add water if needed to completely submerge pears. Cover with lid slightly ajar and simmer, turning occasionally, until pears are tender but not mushy, about 30 minutes.

Using a slotted spoon, transfer pears to a plate. Increase heat and boil poaching liquid until reduced to 1 cup, 10-15 minutes.

DO AHEAD: Can be made 8 hours ahead. Cover and refrigerate pears. Let syrup stand at room temperature. Rewarm syrup before continuing.

Spoon some of syrup over cold or room-temperature pears. Serve with a dollop of crème fraiche or ice cream. Pass remaining syrup.

GF

4th of July Red, White & Blue Fun with Fruit!
Beth Roenker, Seafarer Inn

Ingredients:
Whole watermelon   Shredded coconut
Blueberries

Directions:
Cut the watermelon into slices. Using two or more sizes of star shaped cookie cutters, make star shaped watermelon pieces.

Wash, sort and dry the blueberries.

In a pretty glass bowl or platter, combine the watermelon stars with the blueberries. Sprinkle with coconut.

Notes:
'Fun with fruit' works for other holidays and seasons too. For Valentine's Day, a small heart shaped cookie cutter can make hearts out of strawberries. My favorite is a butterfly – I use it in the summer with watermelon, honeydew and cantaloupe for a garden themed 'fun with fruit!'

GF VG

4th of July
Rockport 4th of July is a trip into the past. The town is alive with Red, White and Blue! The Fireman's Parade, featuring fire trucks, floats, bands and 'horribles', kids and kids at heart dressed as characters, starts at 6 PM at the School (Jerdens Lane.) It continues down South Street and Mt. Pleasant Street, through town onto Main Street and turns onto Beach Street where it ends at the Band Stand at Back Beach. Starting at 8 PM, you are treated to the Rockport Legion Band concert and at 9 PM, a big bonfire on the beach.

Breakfast Energy Smoothie
Debbie Benn, Seven South Street Inn

Ingredients:
2 cups orange juice
1 cup vanilla yogurt
½ tsp vanilla extract
2 cups mixed frozen berries

Directions:
Place all ingredients into blender starting with liquids. I find my VitaMix works best. Blend and immediately turn Vitamix to high, blend until smooth, 30 to 45 seconds.
Top with some fresh berries, serve and enjoy.

Notes:
If you are watching your blood sugar levels, 2 cups of a milk alternative like Almond, Toasted Coconut or soy milk for the Orange Juice. Makes 2-4 Servings.

Orange Julius Smoothie
Debbie Benn, Seven South Street Inn

I discovered that the combination of watermelon and cantaloupe mixed with Sunny D and yogurt tasted just like I remembered from the mall so many years ago.

Ingredients:
1 cup of chilled orange juice or Sunny D
½ cup vanilla yogurt
1½ cups frozen seedless watermelon
1 cup frozen cantaloupe

Directions:
Combine in a high-speed blender or Vitamix on high for about 45 seconds or until desired consistency is reached. Serve in a chilled fluted champagne glass and garnish with a slice of orange.

Banana Split Smoothie
Debbie Benn, Seven South Street Inn

Ingredients:
1 cup milk or soy milk
1 frozen banana
1 cup frozen strawberries
1 cup frozen pineapple chunks
½ cup vanilla yogurt or pineapple cottage cheese
Mini chocolate chips

Directions:
Combine everything but the chocolate chips in a high-speed blender or Vitamix on high for 45 seconds or until desired consistency is reached. Pour into chilled wine glasses and top with a few mini chocolate chips.

Berry Twist
Debbie Benn, Seven South Street Inn

Ingredients:
1 cup orange juice
2 cups frozen berries, total, using any combination of strawberry, blueberry, raspberry, blackberry
½ cup organic vanilla yogurt
½ peeled and de-seeded lime (save the rind, cut into strips to garnish with a twist)

Directions:
Combine all ingredients and process on high in a blender, processor or Vitamix. Pour into chilled champagne flutes and add a twist of lime.

Fall Fashion Smoothie
Debbie Benn, Seven South Street Inn

Ingredient:
1 cup apple juice (not cider)   1 cup frozen seedless red grapes
1 cup frozen cranberries   ½ cup vanilla yogurt

Directions:
Combine all ingredients and process on high in a blender or Vitamix.

Notes:
Add 4 ice cubes if it's too sweet. Share this fall smoothie with a friend. It's sure to keep the cold at bay.

Good Morning Sunshine Smoothie
Debbie Benn, Seven South Street Inn

What a great and refreshing way to start your day!

Ingredients:
1 cup frozen mango (chunks)   1 cup yogurt (my favorite is Stonyfield Organic Vanilla, full fat)
1 cup frozen pineapple (pieces)
1 frozen banana
1 cup orange juice (fresh squeezed or bottled, more or less as needed)   1 scoop of protein powder of choice

Directions:
Add your juice and yogurt followed by your frozen fruit. Blend on high until smooth and add protein powder.

Notes:
If you ever end up making more smoothie than you can enjoy in one sitting, consider pouring the leftover in a popsicle tray and enjoy as a refreshing treat later in the day.

Mango - Coconut Shake-up
Debbie Benn, Seven South Street Inn

Ingredients:
1 large mango, peeled, cubed
1 cup frozen cubed pineapple chunks
½ can coconut milk
½ cup of pineapple juice
4-10 ice cubes to obtain desired consistency

Directions:
Combine all ingredients and process on high in a blender or Vitamix. Pour into chilled wine glasses. Enjoy, it's good enough to be dessert!

VG

Mid-Day Delight
Debbie Benn, Seven South Street Inn

Ingredients:
½ cup of chilled spring water (or pineapple juice)
1 cup frozen pineapple chunks
1 cup frozen green grapes
4 ice cubes if desired.
Hand-full of fresh organic baby spinach

Directions:
Combine all ingredients and process in a high-speed blender or Vitamix. Pour into two 8-ounce glasses and enjoy. I use chilled water in this smoothie instead of pineapple juice because the grapes have a tendency to make it quite sweet. I'm sure something the kids would enjoy.

This is a great afternoon pick me up. When I serve it to guests in the morning, I call it **Morning Dew!**

GF VG

Blueberry & Orange Smoothie
Debbie Benn, Seven South Street Inn

Ingredients:
1 ½ cups orange juice
1 bag of frozen blueberries (2+ cups)
3/4 cups plain or vanilla yogurt (if using plain yogurt add 1 tbsp honey)

Directions:
Combine all ingredients and process on high to desired consistency. Pour into chilled glasses and enjoy.
Turn it into a meal by adding two scoops of protein powder.

Mango - Raspberry Smoothie
Debbie Benn, Seven South Street Inn

Ingredients:
1 cup orange juice
1 cup frozen raspberries
3/4 cup frozen mango
½ cup organic vanilla yogurt

Directions:
Combine all ingredients and process on high to desired consistency. Pour into chilled champagne flutes and top with a fresh raspberry.

Makes 4, 6-ounce servings

Pineapple Pleasure
Debbie Benn, Seven South Street Inn

Ingredients:
1 cup chilled pineapple juice
1 cup frozen pineapple chunks
1 cup frozen strawberries
¼ cup organic vanilla yogurt

Directions:
Combine in a high-speed blender or Vitamix on high for about 45 seconds or until desired consistency is reached. Pour into chilled wine glasses or champagne flutes and garnish with a small whole strawberry on the side of the glass.

The Purple Pineapple
Debbie Benn, Seven South Street Inn

Ingredients:
1 cup chilled pineapple juice
1 ½ cups frozen blueberries (or frozen raspberries or blackberries)
½ cup frozen pineapple
½ cup vanilla yogurt - regular, low fat or fat free

Directions:
Combine all ingredients in a high-speed blender or Vita mix. Turn on low and immediately up to high and process until well blended. Pour into chilled decorative glasses. Serve immediately.

The Paper House
In the North Village of Rockport, known as Pigeon Cove, is an actual house made from newspaper. It was built by Mr. Elis F. Stenman, a mechanical engineer who designed the machines that make paper clips. He began building his Rockport summer home out of paper as a hobby. That was in 1922. The paper was meant to be good insulation. Eventually, not only was the house made of paper, but furniture as well, including a working piano!

Cereals & Yogurts

Lantana House B&B

The Lantana House B&B is an intimate, welcoming Bed and Breakfast open year-round in the heart of historic Rockport, Massachusetts.

Lantana House offers the ultimate in convenience; a strategic location between T-Wharf and bustling Main Street, a mere block from each, yet separated from both. When you want the fun and busy beaches, they're right at hand.

The Inn is one block from the Shalin Liu Performance Center, restaurants, shops and galleries.

And when you want a quiet interlude, the sundeck or covered porch is an inviting and secluded haven tucked away from the world.

Coming to The Lantana House is like 'coming home'.

After a restful, comforting night's sleep, bask in the aromas of freshly baked breakfast goods and exquisitely brewed teas and coffees, before your day at the seashore begins. The Lantana House offers a hearty continental breakfast which consists of home baked goods, house made granola, cereals, fresh fruit, bagels, bread, English muffins, yogurt, hard boiled eggs, meat and cheeses, juice, coffee and tea.

Richard and Tracey are the consummate hosts. They will get you on your way ... to the beach, the sites, adventures, cultural events and even suggest the most picturesque walks.

Lantana House B&B
22 Broadway, Rockport, Massachusetts 01966
978-546-3535
thelantanahouse@gmail.com
www.thelantanahouse.com

Lantana House B&B Granola Recipe

Richard Nestel, Lantana House B&B

Ingredients:
- 2 cups of rolled oats (not instant)
- 1 cup toasted almonds
- ½ cup toasted pecans
- ¼ cup sesame seeds
- ½ cup toasted sunflower seeds
- ½ cup sweetened, flaked coconut
- ½ cup dried cherries
- ½ cup dried cranberries
- ¼ cup canola oil (not olive oil)
- ½ cup honey

Directions:
Preheat oven to 300. Mix the oats, coconut, nuts and seeds in large bowl. Measure oil into a measuring cup and pour into bowl. Measure out the honey in the same unwashed cup. (The oil will keep the honey from sticking to the cup.)

Toss everything together until evenly coated and then pour out into a cookie sheet with a lip (jellyroll pan).

Bake at 300 for 30 minutes. Remove from oven and let stand 2 minutes. Use a spatula to loosen and then allow to cool.

When it is finished cooling, return the baked granola to the mixing bowl, add the cherries and cranberries and stir to combine. ENJOY!!

Notes:
I toast the nuts in a frying pan over medium heat.
This granola is great in a bowl with cold or warm milk, or with yogurt. It makes a great parfait layered with fresh fruit and yogurt.

GF

Orange Zest Granola

Dan Duffy, The Beech Tree B&B

Many of our guests have commented on our granola which we offer as our starter course with fresh seasonal fruit and Greek vanilla yogurt. This unique recipe includes orange zest and molasses within the baked mixture, creating a glazed textured presentation.

Ingredients:
Combine the following in a large bowl:

- 3 ½ cups gluten free oats
- 1 ½ cups gluten free cereal (Corn or Rice Chex)
- ½ cup almonds, chopped
- ½ cup hazelnuts, chopped
- ½ cup pecans, chopped
- ¼ cup pumpkin seeds
- ¼ cup sunflower seeds
- 1/8 cup flax seeds
- 1 cup sesame seeds
- ½ cup dried cranberries
- ½ cup dried apricots, chopped
- ½ cup dried cherries
- ¾ cup flaked unsweetened coconut
- Zest of 1½ orange. Save a small amount to put in liquid pot.

Combine in a small saucepan:

- 1/3 cup molasses
- 1/3 cup maple syrup
- ¼ cup canola oil or flavorless oil
- ½ cup brown sugar
- 1 tsp vanilla
- 2 tsp cinnamon
- 1 tsp nutmeg
- Remaining orange zest and ¼ tsp orange juice

Orange Zest Granola continued

Directions:
Preheat oven to 325.

Combine the first set of ingredients as noted.
Place liquids on medium heat and wait for slow, even boil.

Pour over dry ingredients while stirring. Mix well.

Bake on a baking sheet at 325 for about 8-10 minutes. Turn mixture and return to oven for another 8-10 minutes. Baking time depends on your desired crispness.

Notes:
Can be prepared without nuts for those who may be allergic to them.

Recipe can be halved. Store in airtight container.

GF VG

Lantana
The beautiful and hardy Lantana is the official flower of Rockport.

Tuck Inn Granola

Scott Wood, Tuck Inn

Ingredients:
4 cups dry oats, quick or old-fashioned or mixture
¼ cup brown sugar
¼ cup corn oil

Directions:
Preheat oven to 350. Gradually coat oats with oil. Roast in heavy pan with sides for about 20 minutes, turning with spatula occasionally.

Once cooled, add brown sugar and any high fiber cereal such as All-Bran, Grape Nuts, bran flakes, raisin bran, crushed shredded wheat.

You can also add raisins or other dry fruit such as cranberries or apricots. Crushed walnuts or other nuts are nice too.

GF VG

Maple Pecan Granola

Beth Roenker, Seafarer Inn

Ingredients:

3 cups GF 1-minute quick oats	½ cup coconut oil melted
2 cups pecans, chopped	½ cup maple syrup
1/3 cup sunflower seeds, hulled	½ tsp vanilla extract
¼ tsp sea salt	½ cup craisins
½ tsp cinnamon	¾ cup shredded coconut

Directions:

Preheat oven to 275. Line a rimmed cookie sheet with parchment paper.

In a large mixing bowl, combine oats, pecans, sunflower seeds, salt and cinnamon.

In a measuring cup, combine melted coconut oil, maple syrup and vanilla. Stir.

Pour wet ingredients into dry and stir to combine. Make sure all the oats get wet.

Pour the granola into the pan and spread into an even layer.

Bake at 275 for one hour. Rotate the pan and turn oven up to 300. Bake for an additional 15 minutes. Let cool completely.

Once the granola is cooled, remove from pan and combine in a bowl with the craisins and coconut.

Notes:
This mixture will keep for about three weeks in an airtight container. You will not believe how wonderful this stuff makes the house smell!

GF VG

Stephanie's Hot Quinoa Breakfast Cereal
Stephanie Smith, Changing Tides Bed & Breakfast

Ingredients:
1 cup rinsed quinoa
½ cup diced dehydrated apples
1 cup water
½ cup almond milk
1 tsp cinnamon
3 tbsp maple syrup

Directions:
Combine all ingredients in a sauce pan and bring to a boil.

Reduce to simmer for 20 minutes.

Top with blueberries and toasted walnuts, or your favorite toppings.

GF VG

Roy Moore's Lobster Company
Local dogs love to be walked on Bearskin Neck where they are often swarmed with visitors who want to pet them. They, in turn, want to visit Ken at Roy Moore's Lobster Company where he gives them a tidbit of smoked salmon. Ken's rule: Only one per day.

Overnight Oats

Beth Roenker, Seafarer Inn

Ingredients:
Quick oats (gluten free)	Cinnamon
2% milk	Vanilla
Honey	Fruit

Directions:
In a 5-8 oz jar or glass, pour ¾ cup oats and ¾ cup milk.
Add ½ tbsp honey.
Add a sprinkle of cinnamon.
Add a ½ tsp vanilla.
Stir ingredients.

Add cut strawberries or blueberries or your favorite fruit on top.

Cover tightly and refrigerate overnight.

Serve cold or at room temperature.

Notes:
For a vegan version, substitute coconut milk for the 2% milk and use maple syrup instead of honey.

GF

Yogurt Parfait Bar

Beth Roenker, Seafarer Inn

A really fun idea for brunch or the kids' sleepovers!

Ingredients:
Parfait:

Vanilla yogurt	Cut strawberries
½ tbsp honey	Washed and sorted blueberries

Toppings:

Granola	Raisins
Coconut	Sunflower seeds
Chopped nuts	Chocolate chips
Crushed graham crackers	Cinnamon

Directions:
For each parfait, fill a jar, tall glass or parfait cup 1/3 full with yogurt. Add the blueberries and top the blueberries with ½ tbsp honey. Add another layer of yogurt and top the parfait with cut strawberries.

Set out parfaits with a selection of toppings for guests to add to the parfaits.

Variations:
Parfaits can be made with bananas, papaya, pineapple, apples, raspberries or whatever is in season.

Toppings are endless: nuts like walnuts, pecans, almonds, pistachios; dried fruits like dried cranberries, banana chips, dried apricots; vanilla chips, butterscotch chips, crushed cookies and more.

GF

Savory Breakfasts

The Beech Tree
Bed & Breakfast

Simple Elegance describes the Beech Tree Bed and Breakfast, aptly named for its 150-year-old majestic Copper Beech tree. It is a welcoming landmark to tourists and locals alike due to its prominent location on Broadway. Ideally situated in the heart of Rockport's walkable historic district, the house sits stoically on a hill amidst beautifully landscaped grounds with perennial gardens, natural stone patio and fountains.

In 2001, this private 1850's Greek-Revival home was thoughtfully restored and reconfigured into a charming Bed and Breakfast. Typical Greek-Revival details are evident in the home; the gable fronted façade, portico with Doric columns and entry door surrounded by side lights and upper rectangular transom. Greek influence carries over onto the open columned rocking chair porch, a welcoming retreat for guests. The bright eclectic interior blends period details such as high ceilings, wainscoting, original hardware and leaded glass cabinets with more contemporary features, such as a sunroom with floor to ceiling windows.

Two well-appointed guest rooms and one suite with sitting room have private baths and are equipped with modern amenities for your comfort. Breakfast is served in the sun-filled dining room or on the covered porch or private patio and includes seasonal fresh fruit, Greek yogurt, homemade granola, freshly baked goods, a sweet or savory hot entrée as well as a variety of juices, coffees and teas. Innkeepers, Helene and Dan feel privileged to serve as stewards of this historic home and genuinely love sharing its unique charm with their guests.

The Beech Tree Bed & Breakfast
55 Broadway, Rockport Massachusetts 01966
978-546-2864
www.beechtreebb.com
beechtreebbreservations@gmail.com

Avocado Toast

Helene and Dan Duffy, The Beech Tree B&B

Can't have a New England cookbook without a tribute to the GOAT, TB12, and our fellow Patriots' fans and healthy eaters! For those of you outside of New England, "GOAT, TB 12" is short for the "Greatest of All Time" quarterback, Tom Brady #12.

Ingredients:
2 ripe medium avocados
1 tsp fresh lime juice (helps prevent browning)
1 tbsp EVOO
Salt & pepper to taste
Cayenne pepper to taste
2 slices hearty whole grain bread toasted
Red pepper flakes or preferred toppings

Directions:
In a small bowl combine lime juice, salt, pepper, cayenne and olive oil. Mash the flesh of 1 avocado lightly with a fork, leaving some larger pieces for texture. Add the above oil dressing.

Spread the mixture on well toasted hearty bread of choice.

Slice the other avocado and place slices on top of mixture.

Sprinkle with hot pepper flakes or sesame seeds or whatever you like!

Notes:
"Everything Bagel" seasoning is also great on top.

Zucchini Frittata

Helene Duffy, Beech Tree Bed & Breakfast

Ingredients:
8 eggs
1 small sweet onion
2 medium size zucchini
6 oz grated parmesan cheese
6 oz cottage cheese
½ Knorr's chicken bouillon cube
2 oz light olive oil
½ cup good white wine to your liking (Sauvignon blanc, Chardonnay)

Directions:
Preheat oven to 350. Finely chop the sweet onion.

Wash and thinly slice the unpeeled zucchini (a mandolin works great)

In a frying pan heat up the oil and ½ bouillon cube until it dissolves. Do not use more bouillon as it can be very salty!

Add onions and sauté for about 2 minutes.

Add zucchini and cook until just soft to keep the green color.

Add wine and cook until wine reduces about 1 minute.

Zucchini Frittata continued

In a separate bowl beat eggs add cottage cheese and parmesan cheese and mix together.

When zucchini has cooled mix into the egg and cheese mixture.

Place mixture into a 9-inch glass pie dish.

Bake at 350 for about 30-40 minutes.

Garnish with sour cream and salsa (optional).

Makes 6-8 Servings

Notes:
Our guests like the light fluffy texture of this refreshing summer breakfast dish. I use 1/8 to 1/4 cup of wine. The alcohol evaporates when simmering. I suppose it is optional although I have never made it without it. It is actually more flavorful if allowed to sit a bit. It puffs up, lightly browns and makes a beautiful presentation when sprinkled with Parmesan cheese.

GF

Baked Asparagus and Crabmeat Frittata

Peter Zopatti, The Yankee Clipper Inn

Great for a Springtime brunch!

Ingredients:

2 tbsp fine dry breadcrumbs	½ cup water
1 lb thin asparagus	4 large eggs
1 ½ tsp olive oil	2 large egg whites
1 Vidalia onion, chopped	1 cup part skim ricotta cheese
1 yellow bell pepper, chopped	1 tbsp fresh tarragon, chopped
6 oz fresh lump crabmeat	½ cup shredded gruyere cheese
Salt & pepper to taste	

Directions:
Preheat oven to 325. Coat a 10-inch pie pan or ceramic dish with cooking spray. Sprinkle with breadcrumbs, tapping out the excess.

Snap tough ends off the asparagus. Slice off the top two inches of the tips and cut the stalks into ½ long pieces.

Heat the oil in a large nonstick skillet over medium high heat. Add onions, pepper and cook stirring until softened, about 5 to 7 minutes. Add water and asparagus stalks to skillet reserving the tips. Cook, stirring until the asparagus is tender and liquid has evaporated, about 6 or 7 minutes. (The mixture should be dry.)

Add salt and pepper. Arrange the vegetables in an even layer in the prepared pan.

Whisk eggs and egg whites in a large bowl. Add ricotta and tarragon whisking to blend.

Pour the egg mixture over the vegetables, gently shaking pan to distribute.

Baked Asparagus and Crabmeat Frittata continued

Scatter the reserved asparagus tips over the top and sprinkle with gruyere.

Bake the frittata until a knife inserted in the center comes out clean, about 35 minutes. Let stand for 5 minutes before servings.

For a brunch or dinner, serve with a side salad with a citrus vinaigrette!

The Sandy Bay Breakwater
In 1882, the U.S. Congress authorized a survey of Sandy Bay "with a view to the construction of a breakwater for a harbor of refuge." The goal was to create a massive safe harbor where ships on route between Boston and Portland could duck into in bad weather.
In 1892, after some 500,000 tons of stone had been dumped to form the breakwater's substructure, a final plan was approved for construction of the superstructure. By 1898, crews had completed construction of 600 feet of the superstructure - built of granite stones each weighing an average of six tons - only to have it partially knocked down by a severe storm.
In 1916, 34 years after Congress gave it the go-ahead and with two-thirds of it completed, the construction of the Sandy Bay breakwater was abandoned. By that time, steam power was replacing sail power and the need for a harbor of refuge had diminished. Of the 9,100 foot long breakwater called for in the plans, 6,100 feet were completed. The breakwater remains standing today.
From www.vintagerockport.com, used by permission.

Eggs Benedict with Hollandaise Sauce

Debbie Benn, Seven South Street Inn

Hollandaise Sauce single batch (3 or 4 servings):
Ingredients:
1 stick (¼ lb) of butter at room temperature
3 organic free-range egg yolks
1 tbsp of water
1 tbsp fresh squeezed lemon juice (don't use bottled juice, you won't like the end results)

Directions:
Prepare a double boiler or a glass bowl over a pan of water. Make sure the water is not touching the bottom of the bowl or double boiler. Add the egg yolk, lemon juice and water and mix well using a whisk.

You MUST continue stirring the egg mixture throughout the entire cooking process. Turn on the stove and heat the water up so you have a nice simmer. The eggs will go through several stages while they are cooking. *(If the heat is too high you will start to "cook" the egg yolk and it will appear lumpy. At the first sign of this, remove from the heat to lower the temp of the eggs, all the while whisking as fast as you can. Return to heat.)* First the eggs will get very runny as they start to warm, followed by them getting foamy. After those two stages, you will feel the eggs getting more volume after which they get a nice sheen to them. Then they will also start to pull away from the bottom of the pan as you whisk.

At that point, remove egg mixture from the heat. It is cooked to the proper temperature and ready to accept the butter. Working very quickly, add about ¼ stick of butter and whisk very vigorously. This first insertion is the trickiest and you don't want the eggs to separate. Add another chunk of butter and whisk, continuing until you have incorporated all the butter and you have a beautiful light sauce.

Eggs Benedict   Eggs Oscar   Eggs Florentine

Ingredients:
1-2 fresh eggs per person
1 package of Bay's English muffins (comes in a pack of 6) or sandwich size croissants.

Two slices each of warmed Canadian bacon
Oscar - sautéed asparagus
Florentine - baby organic spinach

At the Seven South Street Inn our guest's favorite is eggs Oscar, and instead of using the traditional English muffin we use croissants.

Directions:
Preheat oven to 350. Put your croissants in the oven on a foil lined baking sheet, and do the same with the Canadian bacon on a separate sheet. Bake at 350 for 10-15 minutes.

Bring salted water with 1 tbsp of white vinegar to a boil in a deep sided frying pan. (The vinegar helps the eggs to stay together.) In the meantime, sauté the vegetables in a frying pan with butter and salt lightly.

Crack eggs into small custard cups and set aside. Slowly pour the eggs, one at a time into the lightly boiling water. Cook until desired doneness but keep in mind that the eggs will continue to cook after they are taken out of the water. Place on a plate and drain well.

To arrange your entrée, place the opened croissant on a plate, add two slices of Canadian bacon followed by the spinach or asparagus and top each with a poached egg. Give the hollandaise sauce a final whisk and put a large spoonful on top of your egg. Place the top half of the croissant lightly over one half of the egg. Serve warm.

Sun-Dried Tomato, Potato Hash w/ Poached egg

Debbie Benn, Seven South Street Inn

We were served this dish at the Beasley House B&B and loved it. The Innkeeper was nice enough to share it with us and we now serve it to our guests.

Ingredients (per person):
- 1-2 jumbo eggs
- 1 red potato medium dice
- ½ small onion, chopped
- ½ tbsp sun dried tomato, chopped
- 1 tsp each butter & EVOO
- 1-2 tbsp crumbled feta cheese
- A pinch (or to taste) of garlic powder, dried parsley, dried basil, dried oregano, salt, pepper and red chili flakes

Directions:
Heat a large sauté pan over medium-low heat and add olive oil and butter. Once the butter is melted & bubbly, add the cubed potatoes and onion. Sprinkle with seasonings. Sauté, turning every 5 minutes until the potatoes are cooked through, about 15-20 minutes. When the potatoes are nearly cooked through, toss in the chopped sun-dried tomato.

While the potatoes are cooking, prepare your poached eggs to your liking.

Arrange your potatoes in decorative ramekins.

Top each with a poached egg and sprinkle with crumbled feta, garnish with fresh parsley when available.

GF

Cape Hedge Sunrise

Debbie Benn, Seven South Street Inn

This is one of our Inn's signatures dishes. I created it especially for my Bed and Breakfast guests.

Ingredients (for one serving. Multiply as needed):
English muffin, (we use *Bay's* found in the refrigerator case of your supermarket)
Haas avocado
Butter, room temperature
Honey ham, thin sliced and cut julienne
Tomato, de-seeded and diced
1 poached egg
Snipped fresh chive for garnish
1 tbsp white vinegar added to frying pan of boiling water with high sides, salted

Directions:
Preheat oven to 350.
Put a handful of julienned ham (per serving) in a loose pile on a baking sheet and put in the oven to warm.

Dice tomatoes, set aside on a microwave safe plate. Cut an avocado in half, remove pit, peel and cut into thin wedges. You will need 4 slices per serving.

Bring pan of water and vinegar to boil. When water is boiling add eggs, one at a time, cooked about 3 min until firm but yolk is still very soft. Remove to a plate. The egg will continue to cook while you assemble the muffin.

Toast and butter a Bay's English muffin per serving. Microwave tomato about 45 seconds to slightly warm but not cook. Place the bottom half of a toasted muffin on desired serving plate, top with fanned slices of avocado, hanging over the muffins edge, followed by the warm julienne ham. Top each with a poached egg and sprinkle a tbsp of warm diced tomato on top of each egg. Garnish with fresh chive.

Puffed Eggs
Debbie Benn, Seven South Street Inn

Ingredients:
½ package of frozen puffed pastry, or 4 squares of pre-cut puffed pastry
4 slices of Havarti cheese
4 eggs, organic and free range, cracked into small custard cups
Salt and Pepper
1 medium sized tomato, sliced, de-seeded and then cubed
4 slices of cooked bacon cut into ½ inch pieces
4 mushrooms, cubed
Fresh cut chives

Directions:
Preheat oven to 375.
Sautee mushrooms in salted butter. Cook bacon. (or use precooked Canadian bacon.)

Cut the puff pastry into 4 squares. Fold the sides of the pastry in about a half inch on all four sides. On a floured surface, flip the pastry over and roll it out to about 5x5 square. Turn right side up. Dust off the excess flour. Place all four on a parchment lined baking sheet and put in the oven. Cook until it is puffing up and turning lightly brown.

Once the pastry is browned (but not cooked) remove from the oven. Place a slice of cheese on each. Using the bottom of the custard cup, make an indent in each pastry to hold the egg.

Sprinkle the tomatoes, cooked mushrooms and cooked bacon around the egg yolk. Return to oven and bake about 10-15 minutes until desired doneness of egg. Top with salt, pepper and chopped chives. Serve.

Ham and Egg Sweet Pepper Rings.
Debbie Benn, Seven South Street Inn

Ingredients:
2 yellow, orange or red bell peppers
8 organic, free range eggs
8 slices of nitrate free turkey, ham or smoked salmon
1 Haas avocado
Olive or avocado oil spray
Sea salt and fresh ground pepper
Fresh herbs for garnish

Directions:
Cut the tops from your peppers and remove the seeds. Slice peppers into 4 ½ inch rings.

Preheat a skillet over medium-high and lightly spray with oil. Place pepper rings in the skillet.

Once the oil starts to sizzle, crack one egg into each ring and turn burner down to medium. Season to your taste and cook until set.

Cut avocado in half and remove the pit. Quarter, then cut into slices.

Fluff a small pile of salmon, ham or turkey on top of egg, followed by slices of avocado.

Cook the eggs to desired doneness, about 3-4 minutes. If you like the top of the eggs cooked more you can place it in a preheated oven for about 5 minutes.

Garnish with your favorite herbs.
Enjoy!

Serves 4

Scrambled Egg Casserole

Debbie Benn, Seven South Street Inn

Ingredients:
8 eggs
½ cup whole milk
Garlic powder, salt & pepper
Butter
2 large handfuls of baby organic spinach
4 medium size mushrooms cut into cubes
1 6-inch piece of kielbasa
Avocado oil
4 slices of Provolone or Havarti cheese

Directions:
Preheat oven to 350.

Prep the eggs:
Beat eggs well with ½ cup of whole organic milk. (I add everything in the Vita mix.) Season egg mixture with salt, pepper and a dash of garlic powder.

Prep the veggies and meat:
Briefly sauté spinach in butter and salt lightly. Sauté mushrooms in butter. Cut the kielbasa into quarters length wise and then cut into cubes and sauté.

Spray a large frying pan with avocado oil. Once pan is heated, add the egg mixture and cook on medium heat until starting to cook but still very soft. (You would not eat them this under-cooked.)

While eggs are cooking, spray 4 small casserole dishes (about 8 oz) with cooking spray, divide the mushrooms, kielbasa and spinach among the four.

Top with the under cooked scrambled egg mixture and add a slice of cheese to each.

Scrambled Egg Casserole continued

Put the casserole dishes on a baking sheet and bake for about 15-20 minutes until eggs are cooked, cheese has melted and it's getting very bubbly around the edges.

When done, remove from the oven and put the casseroles on a plate before serving. Top with your favorite chopped herbs and serve with a multigrain toast.

Notes:
This is a very easy dish to get ready in advance for a brunch. Prepare everything up to the point you put the casseroles in the oven. Enjoy time with your guests and just bake about 20 minutes before you would like to serve. You can also individualize each dish accommodating likes and dislike as well as food allergies because they are all made separately.

Rockport In Bloom Garden Tour
On the last weekend in July, the members of the Rockport Garden Club open their beautiful gardens to the public. This self-guided tour consists of more than a dozen private gardens that celebrate the diverse geography of Rockport, which includes: ocean vistas, enchanting gardens, water features, sculptures and artwork. Lunch is available for purchase at a seaside location. www.rockportgardenclub.org

Tomato Basil Individual Crustless Quiche

Chris & Beth Roenker, Seafarer Inn

This mini-quiche is our most requested recipe!

Ingredients:
12 eggs
1 cup 2% milk
8 oz shredded mozzarella cheese
27 miniature tomatoes such as cherry or grape tomatoes
Fresh basil, 10-15 leaves, chopped
Salt and pepper to taste

Directions:
Preheat oven to 350. Using oversized muffin tins, spray 9 muffin cups with non-stick spray.

Slice tomatoes into halves. Add three half tomatoes to each of 9 muffin cups.

Divide basil and cheese equally into each of the 9 muffin cups.

In a large bowl, whisk the eggs until blended. Add milk, salt and pepper and whisk together.

Divide the egg mixture equally into each of the 9 muffin cups.

Bake for 22 or 23 minutes. Cool for 5 minutes.

Notes:
This is a versatile dish. Instead of tomato, basil and mozzarella, use whatever vegetables you like. Some favorite combinations are mushroom & cheddar; spinach & feta; and zucchini, onion and mixed cheeses.

GF

Egg Baskets

Chris Roenker, Seafarer Inn

Ingredients:
12 eggs
12 pieces of deli ham
1 cup shredded cheddar cheese
Oregano

Directions:
Preheat oven to 350.

Spray a 12 cup muffin tin with non-stick spray.

Line each muffin cup with a piece of ham.

Break an egg into each ham cup.

Sprinkle with cheese.

Sprinkle each with a pinch of oregano (or any fresh herb.)

Bake at 350 for 12 minutes.

Let set for 5 minutes.

GF

Farmers' Market
Every Saturday during the summer and into fall, there is a Farmers' Market in Harvey Park in downtown Rockport. You will find farm grown vegetables, honey, jams, grass fed beef, soaps and more.
www.rockportexchange.com

Layered Hash Brown Pie with Sour Cream and Chives

Helene Duffy, The Beech Tree B&B

This baked hash brown pie is a favorite savory dish of our guests. What distinguishes it from all the rest is the layering of ingredients. A breakfast version of the loaded baked potato.

Ingredients:
3 tbsp olive oil
1 onion chopped
1 pkg hash browns (I use Simply Potatoes)
8 eggs lightly scrambled
½ cup sour cream
Crumbled bacon
1 cup grated cheddar cheese
Green onions or chives

Directions:
Preheat oven to 375.

Brown onions and some of the crumbled bacon in olive oil in a frying pan.

Rinse starch from hash browns and dry. Add to onion mixture and toss.

Spread and bake the hash brown mixture in 2 pie plates or one 7x11 baking dish cooking (spray pans with cooking spray) for about 30 minutes or until evenly brown at 375.

In the meantime, lightly scramble the eggs (not too well done).

Layered Hash Brown Pie continued

Sprinkle the scrambled eggs evenly over the hash browns.

Spread a thin layer of sour cream over the eggs.

Sprinkle crumbled bacon and chives over the sour cream and then the grated cheese.

Bake at 375 degrees for 15 minutes. Watch carefully - do not over bake.
Serves 6-8 people

Notes:
If you like, serve with a small scoop of sour cream.

GF

Movies filmed in Rockport
In 2009, "The Proposal" starring Sandra Bullock and Ryan Reynolds was filmed in Rockport. Dock Square featured a large totem pole and a sign, "Welcome to Sitka, Alaska." Others movies filmed in Rockport include, "Mermaids" starring Cher, "The Love Letter" starring Tom Selleck, Ellen DeGeneres and Kate Capshaw, "Chappaquiddick", "Stuck on You" and the 1988 version of "I'll be Home for Christmas" featuring Hal Holbrook and Eva Marie Saint.

Crabmeat Quiche

Louise Norwood, Rockport Cottage

A favorite of my mother, Cecile Marchildon.

Ingredients:
1 can of good brand crabmeat but fresh is even better
½ cup of mayo
1 tbsp flour
3 eggs beaten
½ cup of half & half
½ cup of scallions
8 oz sharp grated cheese
unbaked pie shell

Directions:
Preheat oven to 350. Fold all ingredients together in large mixing bowl and place in unbaked pie shell.

Bake at 350 degrees for 45 minutes. Remove from oven and allow to set up for five minutes and serve immediately.

Notes:
This quiche is an excellent breakfast, but if you pair it with a salad or grilled asparagus, it makes a terrific lunch or dinner too!

Marion Weinberg's Noodle Pudding
Rosemarie Cerundolo, Periwinkle Cottage

This is my dear friend's recipe and is wonderful as a brunch dish.

Ingredients:
- 10 oz box noodles
- ¾ stick butter
- 16 oz cottage cheese (small curd)
- Small package cream cheese
- ¾ cup (or less) sugar
- ½ pint sour cream
- 4 eggs beaten
- 1 cup milk

Topping:
- 2/3 cup crushed corn flakes
- ½ stick melted butter

Directions:
Cook and drain noodles and add ¾ stick butter melted and set aside.

In a bowl, mix the cottage cheese, cream cheese, sugar and sour cream. Combine noodles and cheese mixture. Pour into greased 13 x 9 casserole pan.

Beat eggs and milk together with 1 cup milk. Pour over noodles. Cover pan and refrigerator 24 hours.

Before baking, combine corn flakes with melted butter and add the topping to the noodles.

Preheat oven 350. Bake 1 hour to 1 hour and 15 minutes. Serve with sliced ham and a green salad.

Notes:
I sometimes add golden raisins or canned peaches (drained) for a sweeter take on this great brunch dish.

Cheese Quiche with Asparagus, Mushroom, Ham Baskets

Debbie Benn, Seven South Street Inn

Ingredients:
1 package of prepared uncooked pie crust (I use Pillsbury when I'm not making homemade)
8 eggs, organic free range
3 cups of half & half
Dash of nutmeg
8-10 slices of Swiss cheese
24 asparagus spears
Salt & pepper to taste
1 14 oz package of mushrooms, sliced
1 lb package Hormel, honey baked ham slices

Directions:
Preheat oven to 350.

Unfold pie crust and roll out. Put in a large pie plate and crimp the edges. Top the pastry with pie weights and bake for about 15 minutes. Remove from the oven and pour out the pie weights.

Working while the pie shell is still hot, line the bottom with the cheese and press into the crust with a fork so it doesn't float.

Blend the eggs, salt, pepper, cream and nutmeg in a blender on low so as not to make a lot of bubbles yet still get it aerated. Pour the egg batter into the pie shell and return to the oven. Bake about 30-45 minutes longer until the crust is golden, and a sharp knife inserted in the center of the quiche comes out clean.

While the quiche is cooking, line muffin cups with about three slices of the honey ham alternating the direction of each slice pressing it all the way into the bottom. Bake in the oven along with the quiche for about 20 minutes until the edges are crispy.

Cheese Quiche continued

Sauté the mushrooms in butter and when the ham baskets come out of the oven, fill each basket with sautéed mushrooms, keep warm.

Sauté the asparagus in butter and sprinkle with a little garlic powder if desired.

When quiche is done remove from the oven and let cool a few minutes. Slice into 8 equal pieces, plate, and top each slice with three fanned out and draped asparagus.

On the stem end that is on the plate, place a mushroom filled ham basket.

Serve with toast of choice and your favorite jam.

Serves 8

Notes:
This entrée is not only a great choice for a Sunday Brunch but also makes a wonderful "Breakfast for Dinner" choice with the addition of a side salad to complete your meal.

Easy Basic Crustless Quiche

Rosemarie Cerundolo, Periwinkle Cottage

Everything but the kitchen sink! Use your imagination!

Ingredients:
Basic Recipe:

4 eggs beaten
1 cup milk
1 cup shredded cheese
1 tsp minced onion

Optional add-ins:
Spinach, broccoli, peppers, onions, tomatoes, mushrooms, bacon, ham, sausage

Directions:
Preheat oven to 350.
Whisk together eggs and milk.   Add cheese and onions and mix well.

Add your choice of vegetables and meats.

Pour into greased pie plate. Bake at 350 for approximately 45 minutes.

GF

Summer Squash & Ricotta Casserole
Helene Duffy, The Beech Tree B&B

Ingredients:
2 large eggs
1 cup mayonnaise
1 cup drained ricotta cheese
1 cup shredded parmesan cheese
2 large eggs
2 cloves garlic (optional)
1 ½ tsp. salt
½ tsp black pepper
2 pounds yellow squash
2 pounds zucchini
2 ½ cups panko bread crumbs
½ cup unsalted butter
2 Tbsp fresh chopped basil for garnish (optional)

Directions:
Preheat oven to 350. In a large bowl whisk together mayonnaise, ricotta, parmesan, eggs, garlic, salt and pepper until smooth and blended. Thinly slice squash and zucchini. A mandolin works best to get it thin.

In a rectangular baking dish alternate layers of yellow and green squash and ¾ of cup of ricotta mixture. It should make about 4 layers depending on size of dish.

Melt butter and mix with panko in a bowl. Spread crumb mixture over casserole and bake at 350 for 30-35 minutes until brown and bubbly.

Let rest for 10 minutes before slicing and garnishing.
Cut into squares, Serves 6-8

Notes:
This can be a tasty breakfast dish or a great side dish for an outdoor barbecue. For the barbecue version, I add 1 teaspoon sugar and use Ritz crackers instead of panko.

Babson Boulder Trail: Walk the Words

During the Great Depression, Roger Babson who founded Babson College, hired unemployed stonecutters to carve over 20 words on the boulders scattered throughout Dogtown. As Roger Babson explained in his 1935 memoir, "My family says that I am defacing the boulders. . . I am really trying to write a simple book with words carved in stone instead of paper." When this Works Projects Administration project was completed, the immense boulders were located in a cleared field. However, over time, nature has reclaimed this field, making the Babson Boulder Trail a fascinating scavenger hunt through the dense woods to rediscover these important life lessons carved in stone.

COURAGE, IDEAS, HELP MOTHER, KINDNESS, LOYALTY, BE ON TIME, GET A JOB, INDUSTRY, INITIATIVE, INTEGRITY, KEEP OUT OF DEBT, SAVE, IDEALS, INTELLIGENCE, SPIRITUAL POWER, STUDY, TRUTH, WORK, BE CLEAN, BE TRUE, PROSPERITY FOLLOWS SERVICE, USE YOUR HEAD, NEVER TRY/NEVER WIN, IF WORK STOPS, VALUES DECAY

The Inns of Rockport Cookbook

Sweet Breakfast

Sally Webster Inn

The Sally Webster Inn has a proud history. It was built in 1832 by Sally's father, William Choate, a housewright. Upon his death in 1859, a share of the property was transferred to each of his 9 children. Sally eventually realized total ownership of the house and it became known as The Sally Webster House. The home became the Sally Webster Inn in the mid 1980's. The Inn is located in Rockport's Historic District.

We are an award-winning Inn recognized as one of the finest accommodations in Rockport and Cape Ann, Massachusetts. The Sally Webster Inn is known for its cleanliness, hospitality, competitive rates and our buffet-style full breakfast. Rooms are antique style with modern amenities.

Chef Sawsan Galal's love of food inspires her to create her own unique "in house" products and breakfasts that cater to each guest's individual tastes and special diets. Hospitality is also at the core of her business. At the Sally Webster Inn, it is all about the relationship that she has with her guests and how she can make them feel at home while on vacation. Inspired by her travels, Chef Sawsan prepares her menu at the Sally Webster Inn with international flavors. Tapping into her wide array of recipes and techniques, she offers a variety of breakfast items daily. Her core philosophy is keep it fresh, keep it local and keep it simple!

Cooking Classes can be scheduled during your stay! Talk to Chef Sawsan to discuss when and what you would like to learn to cook. Guests receive a Special Discount. Cooking has always been a passion with Chef Sawsan, one she loves to share.

Sally Webster Inn
34 Mount Pleasant Street, Rockport, Massachusetts 01966
978-546-9251
info@sallywebster.com
www.sallywebster.com

Delicious Waffles

Sawsan Galal, Sally Webster Inn

Ingredients:

1 cup self-rising flour	½ cup water
1 banana, mashed	1 tsp vanilla extract
1 egg, separated	Pinch of salt
½ cup milk	2 tbsp vegetable oil

Directions:
Mix mashed banana, egg yolk, vanilla and salt in a bowl. Add milk, water and oil and set aside.

In a separate bowl, beat egg white until white and soft peaks form.

Mix banana mixture to flour and mix well. Fold in egg white, making sure you do not over mix batter.

Mixture is now ready to use according to your favorite waffle iron. Prior to using, it is essential that the iron is well preheated and oiled or sprayed with a non-stick spray.

Quick Apple Dumplings
Debbie Benn, Seven South Street

The Inn serves this treat as a breakfast course, but it can be a dessert if you add ice cream or whipped cream.

Ingredients:
- 2 large tart apples, like Granny Smith
- 1 (8 count) package refrigerated crescent roll dough
- ½ to 1 tsp ground cinnamon
- ½ cup butter
- 1 cup of sugar
- 1 cup orange juice
- 1 tsp vanilla extract
- ¾ cup very finely chopped pecans
- Fresh mint

Directions:
Preheat oven to 350. Butter an 8x11 inch baking dish or lasagna pan.

Peel and core apples. Cut each apple into quarters. Unroll and separate crescent roll dough.

Wrap each apple section in a crescent roll. Place the wide end of the crescent just under the bottom edge of the apple and wrap around covering most of the apple and ending with the point on the top of the apple. Sprinkle with cinnamon.

Combine butter, sugar and orange juice in a medium saucepan. Bring to a boil. Remove from the heat and stir in vanilla. Pour the mixture over the dumplings. Sprinkle with pecans.

Bake for 30 minutes, or until the crust is golden and beginning to bubble and the apples are just tender when pierced with a fork.

To serve, place the dumpling in a small bowl or ramekin and spoon the thickened juice and nuts over the top. Garnish with mint.

Blueberry Bread Pudding

Beth Roenker, Seafarer Inn

It doesn't happen often, but some days, we end up with a leftover coffee cake or pile of muffins. When we do, we make the world's best bread pudding from them.

Ingredients:
1 small blueberry coffee cake or
10-12 small muffins
3 eggs, beaten
1 cup milk

½ cup sugar
1 tsp cinnamon
1 tsp vanilla

Directions:
Preheat oven to 350.

Grease a 9-inch square pan. Break up coffee cake (or muffins) into prepared pan.

Combine eggs, milk, sugar, cinnamon and vanilla and pour over broken coffee cake. Make sure all of the cake is moistened.

Bake at 350 for 35-40 minutes.

Serve with maple syrup or whipped cream.

Notes:
This works with a variety of coffee cakes including cranberry, banana or apple cinnamon.

Blueberry Pancakes

Nancy Cameron-Gilsey, The Seaward

Blueberry Pancakes was my absolute favorite breakfast growing up in the Seaward Inn!

Ingredients:
¼ cup flour
½ cup of blueberries
¾ cup milk
2 tbsp melted butter
1 egg

1 cup flour
2 ½ tsp baking powder
2 tbsp sugar
½ tsp salt

Directions:
Dredge ½ cup blueberries in ¼ cup flour.

Put milk, butter and egg in mixing bowl and beat lightly.

Sift together the 1 cup flour, baking powder, sugar and salt.

Add to milk mixture all at once. Stir just enough to dampen the flour. Add extra milk to make the batter about as thick as heavy cream and then add the blueberries.

Pour about ¼ cup mixture on a preheated flat pan or griddle. When batter shows bubbles and the sides are starting to cook, turn pancakes. Cook second side until done.

Serve with butter and syrup.

Lemon Ricotta Pancakes

Helene Duffy, Beech Tree Bed & Breakfast

These pancakes are the lightest, fluffiest pancakes ever and are a good source of protein!

Ingredients:
1 ½ cups flour
3 ½ tbsp sugar
2 tsp baking powder
¼ tsp baking soda
½ tsp salt
1 cup milk (I use 1% but can use whole milk)
¾ cup ricotta cheese (I use part skim but whole is fine)
3 large eggs
1 tsp vanilla extract
1-2 tbsp lemon zest
¼ cup FRESH lemon juice
1 tbsp melted butter

Directions:
Whisk together dry ingredients.

In a separate bowl whisk together milk, cheese, eggs and vanilla until well blended. Add the lemon zest, juice and butter.

Make a well in center of flour mixture. Pour milk mixture into the well. Whisk until combined. Batter should be slightly lumpy.

Pour 1/3 cup batter onto buttered skillet. Wait until bubbles form on surface and one side is golden brown before flipping. Cook other side until golden brown.

Notes:
Fresh blueberries! Rather than putting berries into batter, sprinkle several fresh blueberries onto the individual pancake on griddle before flipping. Berries are more evenly distributed this way. Great with maple syrup or powdered sugar.

Pete's Pumpkin Ginger Pancakes

Peter Zopatti, The Yankee Clipper Inn

Ingredients:

1 ½ cups all-purpose flour	¼ tsp ground ginger
2 tsp baking powder	½ tsp salt
¼ tsp baking soda	¾ cup pure canned pumpkin
2 tsp ground cinnamon	3 tbsp melted unsalted butter
1 tsp ground allspice	1 cup whole milk
¼ tsp fresh ginger	2 large eggs, beaten lightly

Directions:
In a bowl, mix together all dry ingredients. Set aside.

In a large bowl, whisk together the pumpkin and melted butter. Whisk in the milk, followed by the eggs.

Add the dry mixture and whisk until smooth. If the batter seems too thick, add 1 or 2 tbsp water. <u>Do not overmix</u>.

Heat a griddle or nonstick pan over medium heat and coat lightly with vegetable oil.

Drop about ¼ cup batter onto griddle and cook until puffy and bubbling on top – about 2 minutes.   Flip and cook until bottom is done, about 1 more minute.

Serve with maple syrup and powdered sugar.

Makes about 12 pancakes.

Chris' Famous French Toast

Chris Roenker, Seafarer Inn

We have guests who look forward to 'Chris' French Toast' as part of the Seafarer experience! They would be disappointed to go home without at least one morning of French Toast.

Ingredients:

2 eggs	Butter
1 cup milk	1 tsp cinnamon
1 loaf thick French Toast Bread	1 tsp vanilla
(such as Pepperidge Farms)	1 tbsp maple syrup

Directions:
Heat a large, flat pan on medium heat until water drops dance on the surface.

Whisk together eggs, milk, cinnamon, vanilla and syrup.

Dip bread into the egg mixture – about 2 seconds per side.

Coat pan with a pat of butter. When melted, place dipped bread in pan and cook for about 2 minutes. Flip bread and cook 2 more minutes. The bread should be golden brown. (You may need to adjust heat.)

Add more butter to pan and repeat with remaining dipped bread.

Pecan Praline French Toast

Helene Duffy, The Beech Tree B&B

This French toast recipe combines all the rich flavors of classic bread pudding with the fragrant scents of cinnamon, nutmeg and vanilla resulting in a sweet and tasty combination of bread pudding and cinnamon buns! Make it up the night before and set it in the refrigerator overnight.

Ingredients:
- 1 loaf French bread (18 slices)
- 5 large eggs
- ½ cup heavy cream
- 1 ¼ cups whole milk
- 1 tbsp granulated sugar
- 1 tsp vanilla extract
- 1/4 tsp ground cinnamon
- 1/4 tsp ground nutmeg

Directions:
Slice French bread into 18-20 angled slices, 1-inch each.

In a large bowl, combine the eggs, cream, milk, sugar, vanilla, cinnamon and nutmeg. Beat with a whisk until blended but not too bubbly.

Dip each slice of bread into mixture and arrange slices overlapping them into 2 rows in a well buttered 9 x 13 glass baking dish.

Pour remaining egg mixture over the bread slices, making sure all are covered evenly. Cover with foil and refrigerate overnight.

Pecan Praline French Toast continued

Next morning, preheat oven to 350 and prepare the praline topping.

Ingredients:
1 stick of butter	1 tbsp maple syrup
½ cup packed light brown sugar	¼ tsp ground cinnamon
½ cup chopped pecans	¼ tsp ground nutmeg

Melt butter in small pot.

Combine the rest of the ingredients into melted butter. (Heat but do not boil or it will harden and be unusable!!!)

Spread Praline Topping evenly over the bread and with a knife try to get some of the topping between the overlapped slices.

Bake at 350 for 40 minutes, until puffed and lightly golden.

Serve with maple syrup.

Serves 6-8 people

Cape Ann Artisans Open Studio Tour
Twice a year, on the first weekends in June and October, the Cape Ann Artisans open their studios for a self-guided tour of the amazing talent of Cape Ann. You will find wearable art, pottery, mosaics, sculpture, textiles and paintings. www.capeannartisans.com

Orange Crème Brulee' French Toast

Debbie Benn, Seven South Street Inn

Ingredients:

8 eggs, free range and organic
3 cups of half & half
1 loaf of "unsliced" white sandwich bread
1 tsp vanilla
½ tsp of orange extract or emulsion (optional)

Assortment of fresh berries: raspberry, strawberry, blackberry and blueberry
Fresh mint for garnish
Fresh sweetened whipped cream, (optional)
½ cup white sugar (optional for spun sugar*)

Directions:
Preheat oven to 350.
Break 8 eggs into a Vita Mix or large blender. Once the eggs are well-mixed add the flavoring and cream. Mix again briefly.

Cut the crust end off the loaf of bread, measure out and cut slices to 1 ¼ inch thick. Dip each slice of bread into the mixture and put on a sheet pan with sides. Pour the remaining egg mixture over the bread slices. Turn several times until the bread is well soaked on both sides.

Once the bread is soaked, line another baking sheet with parchment paper. Place the soaked and slightly drained bread on the parchment paper and put in the preheated oven. Bake about 12-15 minutes, then check the underside and turn over when the bottom is lightly browned.

Continue baking until both sides are nicely browned and they are very puffed in the middle.

Orange Crème Brulee' French Toast   continued

Working as quickly as possible, arrange a grouping of fruit in the top left corner of each serving of French toast and garnish with mint.

Serves 6

Notes:
When I'm serving this dish at the Inn, I garnish the side of the plate with fresh whipped cream and a little more fruit and add spun sugar* to the top.

*Spun Sugar:
This can be intimidating, and a little tricky to get the right temp to spin the sugar. Just melt the sugar in a dry pan. Do not stir. The sugar will melt and turn amber. Using a wooden spoon, dip the spoon in the sugar and spin it back and forth very quickly until you get the desired thread, then spin over each French toast. If the sugar starts to thicken, put back on the stove until it melts again.

Pineapple Stuffed French Toast with Warm Blueberry Compote

Debbie Benn, Seven South Street Inn

Ingredients:

- 1 loaf of Parisian or a soft style French bread
- 6 large eggs, use 8 if they are smaller
- 1 cup whole milk or half & half
- 1 small can crushed pineapple, very, very well drained
- 1 small brick of cream cheese
- 2-3 tbsp of table sugar
- 1 tsp vanilla
- Cooking spray
- 1 cup of frozen Maine Blueberries
- ½ cup of water, divided
- 1 tbsp of cornstarch
- Powdered sugar for dusting

Directions:

Preheat oven to 350.

Cut the end of the loaf of bread. Cut the loaf of bread every ½ inch, alternating between cutting the bread all the way through. So the first slice cut to about ¼ inch from the bottom of the loaf, the second slice will cut all the way through making a pocket. Continue through the rest of the loaf.

Combine the cream cheese, pineapple and sugar and mix well. Put about 1-2 tablespoons of pineapple mixture in each bread pocket and spread evenly. Set aside.

Mix eggs, milk and vanilla in a blender and pour into a dish. Soak each bread pocket in the egg batter making sure both sides are well soaked.

Spray a frying pan with cooking spray and when heated cook the toast, turning several times to ensure even cooking. When browned on both sides, place in oven for about 10 minutes to make sure they are fully cooked and puffed.

Pineapple Stuffed French Toast with Warm Blueberry Compote continued

While toast is cooking, put blueberries in a small saucepan with ¼ cup of water. Heat to simmer.

Mix one tbsp of corn starch in the remaining water and mix well. Once the blueberries reach the boiling point, turn the heat down and add the corn starch, stirring till thickened. If it is too thick, add a bit of water at a time till you reach desired consistency.

Plate your cooked French toast, about 2 to 3 slices depending on how hungry you are, dust with confections sugar and top with the warm blueberry compote.

Makes about 12 pieces of toast.

The Headlands
The Headlands is a rocky outcrop offering spectacular views of the harbor and the town. Find the entry on either Old Garden Road or Atlantic Avenue. This is a famous place for artists and a great spot for a picnic at sunset or for viewing sailboat races on weekend afternoons.

Orange Marmalade Yoghurt Cake
Helene and Dan Duffy, The Beech Tree B&B

Our largest segment of European guests comes from the United Kingdom. Several of them have told us how much Rockport reminds them of Cornwall, England. We haven't visited the Cornwall County of England, but have seen the coastline and harbor in the PBS Masterpiece Theater production, Poldark. We agree that there are several similarities.

An English couple commented that they enjoyed the Greek yogurt we serve with fresh fruit. They offered to share their orange marmalade yoghurt cake recipe which they thought would complement the Greek yogurt and fresh fruit. We want to share it here with you.

If the measurements seem odd, it is because we converted them from the original recipe, which used ounces.

Ingredients:
For the cake:
½ cup plus 1 tbsp full fat Greek yoghurt
¼ cup vegetable oil
1 lemon-zest only
1 orange-zest only

3 eggs
½ cup plus 1 tbsp caster or superfine sugar
Just under 1 cup flour
2 tsp of baking powder

For cake glaze:
3 ounces of orange marmalade   1 tbsp of orange juice

Directions:
Preheat oven to 350 and grease a 1-pound loaf tin.

In large bowl, beat together yoghurt, vegetable oil, lemon and orange zest and eggs until light and fluffy.

Orange Marmalade Yoghurt Cake continued

Sift in all the dry ingredients and mix until just combined.

Spoon mixture into the loaf tin and bake for 35-40 minutes.

To check whether or not the cake is fully cooked, use a skewer. If it comes out clean, it's done. Remember not to overcook because it will be too dry.

Leave in baking tin a few minutes.

Prepare glaze by warming the marmalade and orange juice until it blends—just a few minutes.
Pour glaze over the cake and leave to cool.

Remove the cake from the tin, slice and serve.

Can be served with fresh cream or yoghurt.

Serves 6-8 people

Almond Croissants (French Bakery Style)

Debbie Benn, Seven South Street Inn

This sweet treat is a perfect size for a breakfast course, which is how I like to serve it at my Inn.

Ingredients:

- 8 med/large croissants (I use the mini croissants from BJ's or your market bakery)
- 4 tbsp dark rum, (I use Myers. This is optional, but highly recommended. You can use 1 tsp vanilla or rum extract instead.)
- 2 tbsp sugar
- 1 cup water
- ½ cup sugar
- 1 cup almond flour
- ½ tsp almond extract
- 1 stick, 8 tbsp butter, room temperature
- 2 large eggs
- Sliced almonds
- Sugar for dusting

Directions:

Syrup:
In a small saucepan, combine 1 cup water, 2 tbsp sugar and rum or extract. Bring to a simmer for a minute and stir until the sugar dissolves, then remove from heat and let cool.

Almond Filling:
Mix almond flour, ½ cup sugar and almond extract, then blend in the butter. Finally add the eggs 1 at a time and mix on med/high speed until the mixture is creamy and fluffy with a frosting-like consistency.

Almond Croissants (French Bakery Style)
contInued

Assembling your French Almond Croissants:
Preheat the oven to 350. Line a cookie sheet with parchment paper. Slice the number of croissants you wish to make horizontally as for a sandwich.

Quickly dip each croissant half into syrup on both sides of the top and bottom pieces. The croissant should be quite moist, but not soaking wet.

Arrange the croissants on a lined sheet pan, cut side up. Spread about 2 Tbsp. of almond filling for large, on the bottom half of each croissant. (About 1 Tbsp. if using the mini croissants.) Place the top halves on. Spread the tops of each croissant with almond filling. Sprinkle with sliced almonds.

Bake on the center rack for 15-18 minutes, or until the cream on top is golden. Dust with a generous amount of powdered sugar.

Notes:
These are best served the same day.
If you are only making a few croissants at a time, store the leftover almond filling in the refrigerator for up to two weeks. Bring to room temperature before using the next time.
For leftover syrup, strain through a fine sieve to remove the pieces of bread and store in the refrigerator.

Basic Crepe Recipe
Stephanie Smith, Changing Tides B&B

Ingredients:
1 cup flour
2 eggs
½ cup milk
½ cup water
¼ tsp salt
2 tbsp melted butter

Directions:
Whisk flour & eggs. Gradually add milk and water stirring to combine. Add salt and melted butter. Beat until smooth.

Heat oiled griddle or crepe pan on medium high heat. Pour ¼ cup batter tilting in a circular direction or spread with crepe spreader so batter is evenly coated in pan. Cook 2 minutes until golden brown and flip to cook the other side.

Strawberries & Cream Crepe Filling
Stephanie Smith, Changing Tides B&B

Ingredients:
1 (8oz) cream cheese, softened
1 ¼ cup powdered sugar, sifted
1 tbsp fresh lemon juice
1 tsp lemon zest
½ tsp vanilla extract
1 cup heavy cream whipped
Fresh strawberries,* cut

Directions:
Blend the cream cheese, confectioner's sugar, lemon juice, lemon zest and vanilla until smooth. Fold in whipped cream.

To serve: fill each crepe with 1/3 cup cream cheese mixture and ¼ cup fresh strawberries. Fold and serve with additional strawberries and a small dollop of whipped cream.

*You can substitute peaches and cinnamon or any fresh fruit.

Gluten Free Vegan Waffles

Sawsan Galal, Sally Webster Inn

Ingredients:
½ cup garbanzo bean flour
1 ½ cups King Arthur all-purpose GF flour
4 tsp baking powder
½ tsp salt
½ cup coconut oil, melted
1 ¾ cup non-dairy milk, slightly warmed
1 tsp vanilla extract
1 tsp apple cider vinegar
2 tbsp agave or honey
½ cup water

Directions:
Mix dry ingredients together. Add remaining ingredients. Mix until all ingredients are well blended.

Mixture is now ready to use according to your favorite waffle iron. Prior to using, it is essential that the iron is well preheated and oiled or sprayed with a non-stick spray.

Yields 6 regular waffles

Notes:
Make the waffles more fun by adding one or more optional ingredients like nuts, fruits, chocolate chips, crumbled crisp bacon.

GF VG

Gluten Free Vegan Chocolate Waffles

Sawsan Galal, Sally Webster Inn

Ingredients:
- 1/3 cup potato starch
- ½ cup King Arthur All-purpose GF flour
- 1/3 cup garbanzo bean flour
- ¼ cocoa
- 1 tsp baking powder
- ½ tsp baking soda
- ½ tsp salt
- 1 flax egg (1 tbsp flax meal added to 2 tbsp water)
- 1/3 cup coconut oil, melted
- 2 tbsp agave or honey
- 1 cup non-dairy chocolate milk (slightly warmed)
- 1 tsp vanilla extract
- vegan chocolate chips (optional)

Directions:
Mix dry ingredients together.

Add remaining ingredients and mix well. Add chips if desired.

Mixture is now ready to use according to your favorite waffle iron. Prior to using, it is essential that the iron is well preheated and oiled or sprayed with a non-stick spray.

Yields 2 large Belgian waffles or 4 regular waffles

GF VG

Waffles
Tobey Shepherd, Linden Tree Inn

Ingredients:
2 cups flour
2 tbsp sugar
1 tbsp baking powder
1 tsp salt
2 eggs separated
1/3 cup vegetable oil
1 3/4 cups milk

Directions:
Sift flour, baking powder, salt and sugar into a large bowl.

Beat together egg yolk, milk and oil. Add all at once into the dry ingredients and mix.

Beat egg whites until soft peaks form. Fold into the batter.

Cook in waffle iron.

Serve with warm maple syrup and butter!

Pebble Beach
Pebble Beach's place in history is secured by the landing of a transatlantic cable here in 1884. James Gordon Bennett, editor of the New York Herald, convinced millionaire John W. Mackay to create the Commercial Cable Company. That company put down two cables from Ireland to Nova Scotia, and two more from there, one to Rockaway Beach, Long Island and the other to Rockport.

Peaches and Cream Wonderful Waffles

Debbie Benn, Seven South Street Inn

This recipe was given to me by my sister in law, Laurie Benn when we first opened in 2000.

Ingredients:
Waffles:
1 ¾ cups flour
2 tbsp sugar
4 tsp baking powder
¼ tsp salt

3 egg yolk
3 egg whites
1 ½ cups milk
1/3 cup oil

Toppings:
½ to 1 pint heavy cream
1-2 tbsp sugar

1 tsp vanilla
1 can sliced peaches, chilled

Directions:
Make the peach sauce: Drain peaches, cut into ½ inch pieces reserving some for garnish and processing the rest in a blender. Process on medium and slowly add some of the peach juice to make a smooth sauce, set aside.

Make the whipped cream: Whip the heavy cream with vanilla and sugar until stiff. Set aside. I place mine in a pastry bag fitted with a large fluted tip.

Make the waffle batter: Sift all the dry ingredients, set aside.

Whip the egg whites until soft peaks form; set aside.

Using an electric mixer, blend all the liquid ingredients in a large bowl, whisk in dry ingredients 'till just blended (don't over mix) then fold in the egg whites (don't over fold.)

Peaches and Cream Wonderful Waffles
continued

Spray your preheated waffle iron with cooking spray. Use a measuring cup with a handle to scoop out the batter. Pour the batter onto a waffle iron and spread out evenly. Cook to manufacturer instructions.

As each batch is cooked place in a 200 degree oven on a baking sheet to keep warm. Finish cooking the rest of the batter.

To plate, garnish the side of the plate with swirls of whipped cream, top with diced peaches and top with peach sauce. For a little color, add a sprig of fresh mint (in season) on the cream or a couple of raspberries. Plate 1 to 2 waffles and top with powdered sugar. Serve warm with real maple syrup.

Notes:
It is extremely easy to double, triple or quadrupled this batter. Any leftovers can easily be wrapped when cooled and then frozen. Perfect for those days when you don't have time to fix breakfast for the kids. Just pop in a toaster or microwave. 1 batch of Belgium waffles yields 8-9 5" waffles.

French Toast Bread Pudding with Spiced Pear Sauce

Tobey Shepherd, Linden Tree Inn

Ingredients:
French Toast:
1 tbsp butter softened
1 loaf bread: cinnamon bread, challah, brioche, or 10-12 large croissants
8 extra large eggs
2 ½ cups milk, or if feeling decadent half & half or heavy cream, or a mix
1 ½ tsp vanilla extract

Spiced Pears:
2 tbsp butter
2 firm ripe Anjou or Comice pears, cored and cut into chunks or 6 canned pear halves drained and chunked
1 tsp sugar
½ tsp ground cinnamon
freshly grated nutmeg
¼ maple syrup plus more for serving

Directions:
The night before:
Prep the French toast: smear butter over the bottom and sides of a 13x9x2-inch baking dish or any shallow 2 quart baking dish. Tear the bread or croissants into small pieces and scatter in dish.

In a bowl, whisk the eggs and sugar 'till light, add the milk and vanilla and whisk well. Pour over the bread evenly. Tamp down the bread with a spoon to submerge all the bread. Cover with foil and gently press foil onto top of bread pudding so that foil is in contact with the French toast. Refrigerate overnight.

In the morning, remove from 'fridge and place into cold oven. Set oven to 350 degrees. Bake 25 minutes and remove the foil. Continue baking until it puffs up and is golden brown, approximately 20 more minutes.

French Toast Bread Pudding with Spiced Pear Sauce continued

While bread pudding is baking, prepare spiced pears. Melt butter in a wide frying pan, preferably non-stick over medium high heat. Add the pears and stir until pears are coated well with the butter.

Sprinkle with sugar, cinnamon and pinch of freshly grated nutmeg. Continue to cook for another 3 minutes until pears begin to soften.

Pour in ¼ cup of the maple syrup. Cook until bubbly and remove from the heat.

Serve bread pudding topped with pear sauce. Have additional maple syrup for extra goodness.

Notes:
Canned pears work well in this recipe because you can get reliable results every time.

Dutch Babies
Helene Duffy, The Beech Tree B&B

Simple ingredients, spectacular results! An unusual name for something light and delectable to eat. And it is not a Dutch recipe. It evolved from the word "Deutsch," hence a German puffed pancake, crisp on the outside, light and tender on the inside. The size of a dinner plate, it serves as a vessel for toppings - sweet or savory - and the presentation always emits a well-deserved "Wow!" It must be served immediately out of the oven as it deflates in a few minutes. It's tricky because of timing, (skillets must be hot!) but worth the experimentation as it uses a few simple ingredients.

Handwerks Oven Soufflé
Debbie Benn, Seven South Street

I have a little story of how we named traditional "Dutch Babies" or "German Pancakes" in our inn. Around 2006, a gentleman from Germany stayed with us. He loved to cook and entertain and collected recipes from his travels around the world. Michael was so taken aback by our Apple version of this dish that he asked for the recipe.

He was a wonderful photographer and so kind and generous. He gave me some of the most beautiful photos of whales that I'd ever seen. In response, we gave him a hand written scroll of the recipe along with a set of pans in which to make it.

His enthusiasm for this dish, as well as his great friendship inspired us to name the dish after him.

That is why we renamed this breakfast, "Handwerks", after our great friend.

Dutch Babies continued

Ingredients:
2 eggs
½ cup whole milk
½ cup flour
1/8 tsp salt

2 tbsp melted butter
Confectioner's sugar and
Toppings of your choice

Directions:
Preheat oven to 475. You will need 2 Individual size cast iron skillets.

Combine eggs, milk, flour and salt until very smooth.

Place individual cast iron skillets on cookie sheet and heat in the oven for about 3-5 minutes. The skillets should be hot but not smoking! The timing and temperature will depend on your oven. Pour melted ½ tsp -1 tbsp butter into each heated skillet to sizzle but not brown.

Pour ½ cup of batter over butter into each skillet and immediately return to oven. Do not burn.

Bake for about 12 minutes until fully puffed and golden.

Remove from skillet and serve immediately with a squeeze of lemon, berries and sprinkled with confectioner's sugar.

Other toppings could be warmed apples and cinnamon, bananas and walnuts with maple syrup or savory bacon bits, grilled ham bits, herbs and cheese. Be creative!

Dutch Babies continued

Notes:
I have seen variations of baking time. Some recipes call for lower temperature and longer cooking time, 425 degrees for 20-25 minutes.
Batter serves 2-3 depending on size of skillet.

Make it Savory:
Scramble two eggs per serving and cook in a frying pan with cooking spray or butter. When eggs are set and a little on the dry side, add crumbles of Herbed Boursin cheese and fold gently until the cheese has melted into the eggs. This will make the best scrambled eggs you have ever tasted.

Spoon eggs into pocket as soon as they come out of the oven and top with some fresh green herbs.

The Inns of Rockport Cookbook

Appetizers

Periwinkle Cottage

An Extra Bed Vacation Rentals is celebrating its 10th year hosting guests from all over the world! We are a year-round, family-owned and operated business specializing in short-term rentals in the Rockport area.

Periwinkle Cottage is nestled on a quiet dead-end street and is walking distance to the village center and Bearskin Neck, the Shalin Liu Performance Center, Front & Back Beach, and the train station. Choose from 2 Town-house style units that have been updated to offer our guests today's modern conveniences with spacious living on two floors. Each unit has a 2nd floor Queen-size Bedroom and 1st floor living space which features a quaint kitchen with stove/oven & refrigerator/freezer, separate heating & cooling, free Wi-Fi, parking, shared laundry and gas grill and private outdoor space with all linens supplied and more!

We offer direct booking on our secure website. Find us at AnExtraBedVacationRentals.com! With direct booking, not only do you save the expense of a costly service fee required by other vacation sites, you are also reserving your stay directly with the owner of the property.

Both units are perfect for a couple for a romantic weekend getaway or a week stay or longer any time of year. Come and experience our warm and welcoming hospitality, our clean and well-maintained units, the quiet and tranquil setting and the many amenities we offer you, our guest, and make Periwinkle Cottage your *"home from home"* on your next visit to Cape Ann.

Periwinkle Cottage... *your "home from home" on Cape Ann*
7 Broadway Terrace, Rockport, Massachusetts 01966
877-325-1139 or 781-820-1513
rosecerundolo@comcast.net
www.AnExtraBedVacationRentals.com

Party Rye Bread Rounds
Rosemarie Cerundolo, Periwinkle Cottage

A party favorite and simple!

Ingredients:
Cocktail Rye Round Bread (from deli area)
Sliced cheddar cheese
Chopped onion (or use dry minced onion with water added to reconstitute)

Directions:
Preheat oven to 350.

Add a slice of cheese to each cocktail rye piece.

Top with chopped onion.

Bake until bubbly.

The Rockport Art Association & Museum
By 1900, many artists were arranging to spend their summers in studios on Bearskin Neck. According to local history books, those early days were communal times. Without modern distractions, the creative community seemed to spend more time just talking. Certainly some of the talk must have been about art for, on July 22, 1921, a group of these artists formed an organization that would support their endeavors.

The RAA&M continues to be one of Cape Ann's most prominent cultural beacons. Since its founding, the Association has steadily increased in size and currently includes approximately 250 artist & photography members and hundreds of contributing members. Each year, the RAA&M hangs over forty diverse exhibitions and offers a variety of educational programs including workshops, children's classes, sketch groups, artist demonstration, gallery talks and artist lectures. www.rockportartassn.org

Sizzling Spicy Shrimp

Sawsan Galal, Sally Webster Inn

Ingredients:

1 lb large shrimp, shelled and deveined
1 fresh red chili pepper
6 tbsp olive oil
2 garlic cloves, minced
Pinch of paprika
Salt to taste

Directions:
Wrap shrimp in paper towels or a clean cloth towel to insure they are dry before proceeding.

Cut the chili in half lengthwise and remove the seeds. Finely chop and set aside. (wearing gloves while working with chili is suggested to avoid any irritation with eyes and hands.)

Heat the olive oil in a large heavy skillet. Add the garlic and cook for 30 seconds. Add the shrimp, chili and paprika. Season with salt. Cook for 2-3 minutes, stirring until shrimp is pink.

Serve shrimp with crusty bread.

Serves 6-8

GF

Smoked Bluefish Pate'

Peter Zupatti, The Yankee Clipper Inn

Ingredients:
- 8 oz cream cheese, softened
- 1 tbsp Worcestershire sauce
- 6 dashes hot sauce
- 1 tbsp fresh lemon juice
- ¼ cup fresh minced chives
- 8 oz boneless, smoked bluefish, flaked
- Toast or crackers for serving

Directions:

In a bowl, blend the cream cheese with all ingredients except bluefish.

Fold the bluefish into the cream cheese mixture.

Garnish with fresh, chopped parsley.

Serve with toast or crackers.

The pate' can be refrigerated for up to 3 days.

Spanish Meatballs in Almond Sauce

Sawsan Galal, Sally Webster Inn

Ingredients:
2 oz white or wheat bread, crust removed
3 tbsp water
1 lb lean ground meat (beef, pork, or combo)
1 large onion, finely chopped
1 garlic clove, minced
2 tbsp chopped flat leaf parsley
1 egg, slightly beaten
½ tsp ground allspice
Pinch of nutmeg
Salt, pepper to taste
Flour for coating
2 tsp olive oil

Almond Sauce:
2 tbsp olive oil
2 oz white or wheat bread, cubed
4 oz blanched almonds
2 garlic cloves, minced
5 oz dry white wine
15 oz vegetable stock
Lemon
Parsley

Directions:
For meatballs: Place bread in a bowl and add water. Let soak for 5 minutes. Squeeze out any excess water and place bread in a dry bowl. Add meat, onion, garlic parsley and egg. Season with salt, pepper, allspice and nutmeg. Knead well to form a smooth mixture.

Spread some flour on a plate. Season lightly with salt and pepper. Using floured hands, shape meat mixture into about 30 equal balls. Roll each ball into seasoned flour mixture.

Heat the olive oil in a skillet and brown meatballs, in batches (4-5 minutes) until browned. Remove from skillet and set aside.

Spanish Meatballs in Almond Sauce continued

To make the sauce:
Heat the olive oil in a skillet and add bread and almonds. Cook gently stirring, until golden. Add the garlic and cook for 30 seconds. Add wine and boil for 1-2 minutes. Season to taste and let cool slightly.

Blend mixture in a processor or small blender with the stock until smooth. Return to skillet.

Carefully add the meatballs and cook gently for 20 minutes until meatballs are tender. Serve with a squeeze of lemon and parsley for taste.

Serves 6-8

Halibut Point State Park
Just three miles north of downtown Rockport, is one of forty quarries mined during the late 1800's. The park got its name from Mariners who sailed its waters in the 17th Century and had to "haul-about" their sails when they reached its outcropping. You can hike around the quarry and on the rocky shore. Check out the tide pools and find hermit crabs and starfish (but don't take them!) On a clear day, you can see Crane Beach in Ipswich, the Isles of Shoals off the coast of New Hampshire and all the way to Mount Agamenticus, located 81 miles away in Maine.

Carrot and Toasted Almond Dip

Sawsan Galal, Sally Webster Inn

Ingredients:
1 lb carrots, sliced into ½ inch pieces
½ cup sliced almonds, toasted
Salt and pepper to taste
¼ cup olive oil
2 garlic cloves

Directions:
Bring one quart of water with carrots to a boil. Cook until carrots are very soft. Drain.

Place in a food processor with remaining ingredients. Process until smooth.

Cool and serve with pita chips or fresh vegetables as a dip.

Notes:
If dip is too runny, add plain breadcrumbs (can be gluten free), one tbsp at a time, allowing a few minutes between each addition for the crumbs to thicken the dip.

GF VG

Game Day Kielbasa

Beth Roenker, Seafarer Inn

In the fall, we gather every *Game Day* for a pot luck football party. This is one of my favorites and a crowd pleaser.

Ingredients:
2 packages kielbasa   ½ cup water
½ cup barbecue sauce

Directions:
Cut kielbasa into ½ rounds.

In a nonstick frying pan, brown the kielbasa. Add the barbecue sauce and water and mix well.

Boil off the water, stirring often, until the barbecue sauce glazes the kielbasa.

Serve with mustard or barbecue sauce for dipping.

Go Pats!

Artichoke Dip

Helene and Dan Duffy, The Beech Tree B&B

Guests will gobble up this hot, creamy appetizer served with your favorite chip or cracker.

Ingredients:

1 cup Hellmann's mayonnaise	1 clove minced garlic
1 cup shredded parmesan	1 can artichoke hearts, drained
1 cup shredded mozzarella	and water pressed out

Directions:
Preheat oven to 350.

Finely chop the artichoke hearts and combine with other ingredients.

Bake in a shallow casserole dish at 350 for 20-25 minutes until top is nicely browned.

GF

Feta Cheese and Tomato Spread

Sawsan Galal, Sally Webster Inn

Ingredients:

1 lb feta cheese	¼ tsp dry mint, crushed
2 tomatoes, minced	olive oil to taste, 1-3 tbsp
½ tsp lemon juice	pita bread chips

Directions:

With a fork or in a food processor, crumble feta cheese into fine pieces. Remove to a clean bowl.

Add tomatoes and other ingredients.

Mix well and serve with pita chips or as an accompaniment to any good bread.

*** The Back Beach American Legion Bandstand***
The Bandstand is a taste of old time comfort. On Sunday evenings throughout the summer, enjoy an old-time band concert and, on Mondays, listen to "Music on the Beach" provided by local bands and singers. It is also the best seat in the house for the July 4th bonfire and the August fireworks.

Cheese Log
Lynne Norris, Pleasant Street Inn

Ingredients:
2 lb Velveeta
1 ½ lb natural cheddar cheese (mild or sharp)
½ to 1 lb blue cheese
½ cup Heinz sweet relish
1 whole onion grated
2 tsp horseradish
1 tbsp Worcestershire sauce
2 tbsp French's mustard
Coarsely ground nuts (walnuts or pecans)

Directions:
Allow cheeses to reach room temperature, then mix all ingredients (except nuts) together using an electric mixer.

Form mixture into 4 logs and roll each in coarsely ground nuts of your choice.

Serve with crackers, fruit or bread.

Notes:
The logs can be frozen!

Cranberry Pecan Mini Goat Cheese Balls

Tobey Shepherd, Linden Tree Inn

Ingredients:
16 oz cream cheese softened
8 oz goat cheese

½ cup roughly chopped dried cranberries
½ cup finely chopped pecans

Coating:
½ cup or more chopped dried cranberries

30 pretzel sticks

Directions:
Combine the cheeses, ½ cup cranberries and ½ cup pecans in a large bowl, stirring until combined.

Using a small cookie scoop or spoon, form small balls, rolling them using your hands.

Place remaining chopped dried cranberries in a shallow bowl and roll goat cheese balls in the coating.

Place pretzel stick in each ball.

Refrigerate until ready to serve. Serve with assorted crackers and pretzels.

Notes:
If preparing more than 4 hours ahead of serving, don't add the pretzel sticks until serving time.

Dogtown or Dogtown Commons

Once known as the Common Settlement, the area later known as Dogtown is divided between the city of Gloucester and the town of Rockport. Dogtown was first settled in 1693 and, according to legend, the name of the settlement came from dogs that women kept while their husbands were fighting in the American Revolution. The community grew to be 5 square miles and was an ideal location as it provided protection from pirates and enemy natives. By the early 1700s, the land was opened up to individual settlement as previously it had been used as common land for wood and pasturing cattle and sheep. It is estimated that at one point 60 to 80 homes stood in Dogtown at the peak of its population. In the mid-1700s as many as 100 families inhabited Dogtown which remained stable until after the American Revolution. Various factors led to the demise of Dogtown which included a revived fishing industry from Gloucester Harbor after the American Revolution had ended. After its abandonment, Dogtown was a mostly cleared open field with abundant boulders around. Nearby residents used this land to graze their farm animals. These animals were kept in private lots into the 1920s when the last of the plots were abandoned. In the decades that followed, what was once open land eventually became a dense forest. Dogtown is now a favorite spot for dog walkers and nature lovers.

Soups

The Yankee Clipper Inn

The Yankee Clipper Inn is a 1929 art deco mansion that sits on a rocky bluff overlooking the picturesque Atlantic Ocean in the quintessential seaside town of Rockport, Massachusetts. Our Inn is conveniently located 3/4 of a mile from beaches and downtown Rockport. The Inn is conveniently located 35 miles north of Boston with a total of 15 guest suites, 8 suites ocean-front in our main Yankee Clipper building and 7 suites across the street in our Historic Bulfinch House. Most of the guest rooms in both buildings provide spectacular ocean views. The Inn offers an ocean-front function room and a patio available for weddings, business meetings or other special events. Our famous guest list includes such icons as President John F. Kennedy, John Lennon, Paul Newman, Bette Davis, June Allison and countless others.

The Yankee Clipper Inn has won countless awards over the years. Arrington's Bed and Breakfast Journal has voted the Yankee Clipper Inn as "The best inn on the eastern seaboard," "One of the best inns in the country," and "Most panoramic ocean views." Boston Magazine named the Yankee Clipper Inn "Best Nearby Escape." The inn has been featured in Country Living Magazine and on The Country Inns television program and North Shore Magazine's 2012 Editor's Choice Best Bed & Breakfast.

Spacious, manicured grounds and flower gardens surround this great Rockport inn. Guests can sit and relax on our oceanfront patio or spend a quiet moment in the oceanfront gazebo, overlooking the Atlantic Ocean and the town of Rockport. A salt water pool is located on the property for guests to enjoy.

Yankee Clipper Inn...*where memories are made.*
127 Granite Street, Rockport, Massachusetts 01966
978-546-0001
yankeeclipperinn@gmail.com
www.yankeeclipperinn.com

Butternut Squash Bisque with Cornbread Croutons & Blue Cheese Crumbles

Peter Zopatti, The Yankee Clipper Inn

Ingredients:
1 quart vegetable broth
¼ cup melted unsalted butter plus 2 tbsp
½ cup chopped leek (white part only)
3 butternut squash
¼ tsp cinnamon
¼ tsp allspice
Salt and pepper to taste
¼ cup heavy cream

Directions:
Preheat oven to 450. Cut squash in half and scoop out seeds. Generously brush the squash with ¼ cup melted butter, sprinkle with spices, salt & pepper.

Place squash in a roasting pan, cover with foil and roast 35 – 40 minutes or until tender when pierced with a fork.

When cool enough to handle, scoop flesh into a bowl, add ½ quart of broth and set aside.

In a stockpot, cook leeks in remaining 2 tbsp butter until soft, about 6 minutes over medium heat. Add reserved squash and broth plus remaining broth and bring to a boil, then reduce heat and simmer over medium low about 30 minutes. Puree soup either in a blender or with infusion blender until smooth. Season with salt and pepper. Add heavy cream to finish bisque.

Garnish with corn bread croutons and crumbled blue cheese. Thinly sliced prosciutto also adds another dimension!

Notes:
If soup becomes too thick, add 2 tbsp water at a time until desired thickness.

GF

Chilled Mango Cucumber Soup

Peter Zopatti, The Yankee Clipper Inn

Ingredients:
3 mangos, peeled and pitted
3 seedless cucumbers
3 tbsp finely chopped red onion
3-4 tbsp fresh lime juice
3 tbsp fresh chopped cilantro
Sea salt & pepper
2 tsp diced jalapeno pepper (optional)

Directions:
Finely chop 1 mango and 1 cucumber and set aside.

Coarsely chop remaining mangos and cucumbers and puree with ¼ cup water in a blender until smooth.

Transfer to a bowl and stir in finely chopped mango and cucumber. Add 1 tsp sea salt and pepper. Add jalapeno if you like it hot.

Stir in cilantro just before serving.

GF VG

Rockport Acoustic Music Festival
Over 3 decades ago, friends got together to play some music in the park across from the beach in "the meadow," with a view of the ocean, some swings and a slide... yeah, that place with the waterfall and the bridges over the streams. Nice. Since 1979, the festival, held the first weekend in August, has brought performers from many genres—acoustic rock, folk, world, blues, jazz, Celtic, bluegrass, world vibe and more—from across the country to perform during the peak of our summer season in Rockport, Massachusetts. www.rockportusa.com/events-festival

Celery Root Potato Soup
The Emerson Inn

Ingredients:
10 lb celery root, washed, peeled, and diced
4 Yukon gold potatoes, washed, peeled, and diced
1 Spanish onion, julienned
2 leeks, washed, sliced thin
4 quarts vegetable stock
2 quarts cream
1 pint white wine
Salt and Pepper to taste

Directions:
In a large heavy bottom pot, heat oil on medium heat. Add onions and leeks, sweat for 3-4 minutes, do not allow to brown.

Deglaze with white wine. When wine is reduced, add potatoes and celery root, season appropriately. Let vegetables cook on medium low heat for 5 minutes stirring occasionally.

Add vegetable stock, bring to a boil, let simmer for 1 hour.

When vegetables are tender, add heavy cream and let simmer for 30-40 minutes.

Remove from heat, <u>do not strain</u>; puree soup in Vitamix, in batches, adjust seasoning as necessary.

GF

Best Ever Vegetable or Chicken Bone Broth

Debbie Benn, Seven South Street Inn

Ingredients:

1 large onion, or two medium, roughly chopped
6 celery stalks, roughly chopped
3 carrots, roughly chopped
4 cloves garlic, crushed
3 bay leaves
1 tbsp Italian herbs or 1 tsp each thyme, rosemary, oregano
2 tbsp sea salt
1 tsp whole pepper corns
1 tsp turmeric powder or 1 tbsp fresh turmeric
1 tsp ginger powder or 1 tbsp fresh ginger, chopped
3 quarts of water
2 tbsp apple cider vinegar
1 large chicken or chicken carcass if making chicken broth

Directions:
Add onion, celery, carrots, garlic, bay leaves, herbs, salt, pepper, turmeric, ginger and water in a large Dutch oven or slow cooker. If making chicken broth, add chicken and vinegar.

If you're making the vegetable broth, slow cook or simmer for 2-4 hours. If you're making the chicken broth, slow cook for 6-10 hours and add apple cider vinegar. If using a whole chicken, remove chicken when cooked and remove meat and return the carcass to cooker.

Strain the liquid. Allow to cool.

Notes:
Serve as is or use as base for any soups or stews.
Broth can be saved for up to 3 days in the refrigerator.
Freeze any unused portion for later use, up to 6 months.

Vegan Cream of Broccoli Soup

Tobey Shepherd, Linden Tree Inn

This recipe is paleo and grain free!

Ingredients:
1 tsp extra-virgin olive oil
1 yellow onion, sliced
1 tsp sea salt
Freshly ground pepper, to taste
3 cups unsweetened almond milk
4 cups cauliflower florets (1 medium head of cauliflower)
3 cups broccoli florets, finely chopped
1 tbsp onion powder

Directions:
Sauté onion in oil over medium high heat in a medium saucepan for 5 minutes, adding a few tbsp of water to keep from burning!

Add cauliflower and milk. Cover and bring to a boil, reduce heat and simmer covered for 10 minutes or until cauliflower is soft. Add in half of the broccoli. Puree. (If using a high powered blender or food processor put the mixture in a bowl and puree till smooth, then return to pot. Alternately, you can also use an immersion blender. Remove pan from heat and puree with the blender till smooth.)

Stir in remaining broccoli and onion powder. Cover and cook for another 10 minutes until thickened.

Serve immediately.

Notes:
The onion powder really enhances the taste of the soup, so even though it seems odd, it really does need it.

GF VG

Thai Style Chicken Soup

Peter Zopatti, The Yankee Clipper Inn

Ingredients:

2 tsp oil
1 tbsp red curry paste (such as Taste of Thai brand)
1 garlic clove, crushed
1 large red onion, diced
1 quart chicken stock
1 can coconut milk
1 lb boneless chicken thighs, cut into bite sized pieces
3 tbsp Thai fish sauce
1 tsp sugar
1 cup frozen peas
4 tbsp chopped cilantro
1 tbsp fresh lime juice

Directions:

Heat oil in a large saucepan or stock pot. Add the onion, garlic and curry paste and cook for about 2 minutes, stirring constantly over medium heat.

Stir in the stock and coconut milk and bring to a boil over medium high heat.

Add the chicken, fish sauce and sugar. Lower the heat and simmer, covered for 15 minutes, stirring occasionally.

Add the peas and lime juice and cook for 2 minutes longer. Stir in cilantro just before serving.

Serves 8

New England Clam Chowder

Beth Roenker, Seafarer Inn

Ingredients:
- 4 slices bacon, chopped
- 1 onion, chopped
- 4 stalks celery, chopped
- 1/3 cup flour (optional)
- 1 tsp pepper
- 1 tsp thyme
- 5 cans minced clams with juice
- 1 ½ cups chicken stock
- 2 large potatoes, peeled and cubed
- 2 cups heavy cream
- 1 bay leaf

Directions:

Drain the clams and reserve the juice.

In a large soup pot, fry the bacon until fat renders and edges start to crisp. Add onion and sauté until softened, about 4 or 5 minutes.

Reduce heat to low and add celery, and, if you like a thicker chowder the flour, stirring constantly for 3-5 minutes.

Add the bay leaf, pepper, thyme, clam juice, chicken stock and stir. Add the potatoes and bring to a boil. Reduce heat to simmer and cook until the potatoes are done.

Remove bay leaf and add cream. Allow soup to simmer and thicken.

Add in clams and heat through.

Serve with oyster crackers and a green salad.

Cream of Tomato Soup

Sawsan Galal, Sally Webster Inn

Ingredients:
4 tbsp unsalted butter
1 slice bacon, finely chopped
1 Spanish onion, chopped
1 carrot, chopped
1 stalk celery
4 cloves garlic, finely chopped
5 tbsp all-purpose flour
4 ½ cups low-sodium chicken broth
1 28 oz can whole, peeled tomatoes
3 parsley sprigs
3 fresh thyme sprigs
1 bay leaf
1 cup heavy cream
1 3/4 tsp kosher salt
Freshly ground black pepper

Directions:
Heat the butter in a large soup pot over medium-high heat. Add the bacon and cook, stirring, until crisp and most of the fat has rendered, about 1 minute. Using a slotted spoon, transfer the bacon to a paper towel-lined plate and set aside.

Lower the heat to medium, add the onion, carrots, celery and garlic and cook, covered, stirring occasionally, until soft and fragrant, about 8 minutes.

Stir in the flour and cook, stirring, for 3 minutes.

Pour in the broth and crush the tomatoes through your fingers into the pan. Bring to a boil while whisking constantly.

Tie the parsley sprigs, thyme and bay leaf together with a piece of kitchen twine and add to the pot. Lower the heat and simmer for 20 minutes. Remove from the heat and let cool.

Cream of Tomato Soup continued

Remove and discard the herb bundle.

Working in batches, transfer the mixture to a blender and puree until smooth. Return the puree to the pot and reheat over medium heat.

Whisk in the heavy cream, salt and pepper, to taste. Divide among warm soup bowls and serve immediately.

Old First Parish Burying Ground
Rockport's oldest cemetery is across the street from Front Beach. Many family members of Rockport's earliest settlers are buried in this historic cemetery, including the Tarr, Poole and Hale families, as well as famous daughter, Hannah Jumper, a leader of the 1856 Rockport Temperance movement. First settler, Richard Tarr was buried here in 1732. Also buried here are officers and soldiers of the French and Indian, Revolutionary and 1812 wars.

Corn Chowder

Sawsan Galal, Sally Webster Inn

Ingredients:
2 tbsp butter
EVOO
1 onion, diced
2 garlic cloves, minced
6 sprigs fresh thyme, leaves only
¼ cup all-purpose flour
6 cups canned vegetable stock
2 cups heavy cream
2 Idaho potatoes, peeled and diced
6 ears corn
Salt and freshly ground black pepper
¼ cup chopped fresh parsley

Directions:
Heat the butter and 1 tbsp olive oil in a soup pot over medium heat. Add the onion, garlic and thyme and cook until the vegetables are good and soft, 8-10 minutes.

Dust the vegetables with flour and stir to coat everything well. Pour in the vegetable stock and bring to a boil.

Add the cream and the potatoes, bring to a boil and boil hard for about 7 minutes, until the potatoes break down (this will help to thicken the soup and give it a good texture).

Cut the corn kernels off the cob and add to the soup. Season with salt and pepper and simmer until the corn is soft, about 10-12 minutes. Stir in the parsley and give it another little drink of olive oil.

Ladle the soup into bowls and serve.

Crock-Pot Beef Barley Soup
Beth Roenker, Seafarer Inn

Ingredients:

1 ½ lb stew meat	6 cups water
2 chopped carrots	2 bay leaves
3 stalks chopped celery	2/3 cup barley
1 chopped small onion	Salt and pepper
2 cloves chopped garlic	Thyme

Directions:
Brown beef.
Put everything in a crock-pot.
Cook for 6 hours on high.

OR:
Brown beef.
Add everything to a soup pot.
Boil, reduce heat to low and cover.   Simmer covered about 1 ½ to 2 hours.

No Stoplights
Did you know that Rockport has no stoplights or neon signs?

Delicious Chicken Taco Soup
Debbie Benn, Seven South Street Inn

Ingredients:
2 tbsp avocado oil
1 large diced sweet onion
1 large clove garlic, crushed, then chopped fine
1 can black beans, drained
1 can light kidney beans, drained
1 small can tomato sauce
2 cans diced tomatoes with or without green chilis
1 tsp cumin
1 tsp chili powder
2 boneless, skinless chicken breasts
1 cup chicken broth or water
1 bag frozen whole kernel corn
1 tbsp taco or chili seasoning

Optional ingredients:
Shredded cheese of choice (I like a Mexican blend)
Sour Cream
1 cup Chili Mac pasta: cooked, drained, rinsed and set aside.

Directions:
Preheat oven to 350. Sauté onions in a Dutch oven with 2 tbsp of avocado oil until opaque, add chopped garlic and sauté a few minutes longer.

Add the rest of the ingredients to the pot with the onions and cover. Cook in oven for about one hour.

Remove the chicken to a cutting board and using two forks, shred the chicken and then return it to the pot. If you are using Chili Mac you should add it to the soup at this time.

Stir and serve with grated cheese and a dollop of sour cream.

You can also make the vegetarian version of this dish; just omit the chicken.

My Best Ever Coconut Curry Soup with Shrimp

Debbie Benn, Seven South Street Inn

This is the fastest soup to make, have it on the table in about 45 minutes and oh, so good. This recipe can easily be doubled to have for lunch throughout the week.

Ingredients:
2 cans of full-fat coconut milk
1 cup of chicken bone broth or vegetable broth
1 cup chopped cauliflower
1 cup chopped organic baby spinach
1 cup chopped sweet onion
1 tbsp fresh grated ginger
1 clove garlic, minced
2 tbsp coconut oil or MCT oil
1 tbsp curry powder
1 tsp turmeric powder
½ tsp Himalayan pink salt
½ package of brown rice noodles
1 ½ cups of small shrimp cut in half
1 small sweet potato peeled and diced into small bite size cubes (optional)

Directions:
Heat oil in medium sauce pan and add onion, garlic and ginger, (and sweet potato if using). Sauté over low heat until vegetables are tender. Add coconut milk, broth, cauliflower, curry powder, turmeric and salt to pan. Stir well and often.

In the meantime, cook a half package of broken up rice noodles in salted water to al dente, drain and rinse.

Cook over medium heat for about 10 minutes. Lower heat to simmer and cook about 10 more minutes. Then add spinach, rice noodles and shrimp and simmer about another 5 minutes.

Serve with a mixed greens salad with an Asian dressing.

There are two holidays you can only celebrate in Rockport.

Motif #1 Day
Motif #1 Day happens on the third Saturday in May in honor of the fishing shack, artist's studio and tourist attraction in the center of Rockport Harbor, a building painted so often by artists at the turn of the last century that it was given the nickname Motif #1. The festival celebrates the arts in Rockport with film, poetry, dance, music, art and more and even includes a 5k and fun run. www.rockportexchange.com

Illumination Night
Illumination Night is celebrated the second Saturday in August. The whole town illuminates the night with lanterns hung everywhere you look. The highlight of the day is the fireworks set off Granite Pier after the sun sets. The best seat in the house is at Back Beach, where, all afternoon, the Rockport Rotary club hosts its annual Lobster Fest, serving a traditional lobster bake on picnic tables by the Bandstand. It's a summer day you will never forget. www.rockportilluminations.com

Main Dishes

Linden Tree Inn

The Linden Tree Inn is a charming 1850 Victorian Bed & Breakfast Inn. Originally built as a single family home, the Linden Tree has been in continuous use as an inn since the 1920's. Tobey and John have been the owners and innkeepers since 2002 and enjoy hosting guests year round, and small retreat groups and family reunions during the quiet months.

Our guest rooms are individually decorated, all with private bath. The Carriage House features 4 large modern rooms. Carriage House units have a semi-efficiency kitchenette and are ideal for small families or longer stays.

Enjoy our full home-cooked breakfast including Tobey's "legendary melt-in-your-mouth" scones each day. The inn is non-smoking for your comfort. Tobey and John believe their inn is the perfect place for rest, relaxation and romance, and can comfortably meet the needs of singles, couples or small families. During the warm months guests can relax on the deck or under the linden tree, where there is always a gentle breeze.

We have a large parking lot on site, park up when you arrive and then walk to most of what Rockport has to offer. Located on a quiet residential side street, the Linden Tree is just a short walk to the beach, restaurants and over 100 unique shops. Across the street is Millbrook Meadow and Pond to explore and enjoy.

Come and experience for yourself our Anglo-American hospitality!

The Linden Tree Inn
26 King Street, Rockport, Massachusetts 01966

Shepherd's Pie
Tobey Shepherd, Linden Tree Inn

This recipe feeds a crowd of about 10 or fewer really hungry people!

Ingredients:

4 pounds of ground meat, beef or turkey	4 cans corn drained or frozen corn
Olive or vegetable oil	6 pounds potatoes
2 onions	

Directions:
Heat oven to 375.
In a cast iron skillet, sauté onions and ground meat in olive oil or your choice of vegetable oil. (I usually use ground turkey to make the dish healthier.)

When meat is cooked, add in corn.

Boil potatoes in salted water till cooked then drain, mash with butter and milk. Cover the meat mixture with the mashed potatoes. (If not using a cast iron skillet or oven-proof skillet, place meat and corn in an oven-proof baking dish. Spread mashed potatoes on top of meat and corn mixture.)

Place in heated oven and bake 20 minutes or so until top is slightly browned and mixture is bubbly. Serve with salad and bread.

Notes:
I always tell guests that this is our signature dish, and that no Shepherds were harmed in the making of their dinner!
When I make this for 2, I use one pound of meat, 1 can of corn, 1 onion and about a pound or two of potatoes. I really like using the little thin skinned potatoes, no need to skin them.

GF

Sawsan's Bolognese Sauce

Sawsan Galal, Sally Webster Inn

Ingredients:
1 cup diced carrots
1 cup diced onions
1 cup diced celery
¼ cup olive oil
4-5 garlic cloves, minced
1 ½ lbs sweet (or hot) Turkey Italian Sausage (out of casing)
1 ½ lbs ground beef
3 6 oz cans tomato paste ***14 oz can crushed or diced tomatoes ***
1 cup hardy red wine
1 tsp ground allspice
1 tsp fennel seeds
water
2 tbsp chopped parsley

Directions:
In a large saucepan, sauté onions, carrots and celery in oil 'till soft. Add crushed garlic and only cook for 30 or so seconds.

Add meat and, while breaking up the meat with a wooden spoon, cook through.

Add allspice and fennel seeds, tomato paste, red wine and crushed tomatoes, along with ½ cup of water. Stir to dissolve the paste and mix all ingredients together.

Simmer on medium to low heat until raw tomato flavor is gone. Finish with chopped parsley.

Notes:
Add small amounts of water if more cooking is needed.
***The tomato items can be substituted with about 4 cups tomato puree.

Taco Casserole
Beth Roenker, Seafarer Inn

Ingredients:
1 lb ground turkey
Medium onion – chopped
1 can tomatoes with green chilies (such as Rotelle)
1 can refried beans
2 fresh tomatoes, chopped
2 cups spinach, chopped
1 package taco seasoning
Water per package directions

Directions:
Preheat oven to 350. Brown the ground turkey with the onions in a bit of olive oil. Add the taco seasoning with water and mix.

Grease a small casserole dish.

Pour the turkey mixture into the casserole dish.
Top with chopped tomatoes and spinach.

Mix the refried beans with the canned tomato and chilies.
Top the casserole layers with the mixed beans.

Cook at 350 for 40 minutes.

Serve with fresh chopped lettuce and tomatoes and taco sauce or salsa.

Notes:
Add tortilla chips if desired or top the beans with shredded cheese before baking.

Chicken Stew for Two

Beth Roenker, Seafarer Inn

Ingredients:

1 large boneless, skinless chicken breast
¼ cup flour
1 tbsp olive oil
1 tbsp thyme
1 tbsp sage
Salt and pepper to taste
15 oz chicken broth
¼ cup dry red wine
1 bay leaf
1 chopped carrot
4 or 5 asparagus cut into small pieces
1 small head of broccoli, cut into small pieces and including stems
6 stalks of celery, chopped
1 onion, chopped
1 can of corn

Directions:
Cut the chicken into bite sized pieces.

Put chicken pieces, flour and herbs in a plastic bag and shake to cover chicken pieces with herbed flour.

Brown the chicken pieces in oil.

Add the chicken broth, wine and bay leaf with salt and pepper to taste. Add the carrots, asparagus, celery and onion.

Simmer for ½ hour until carrots are soft.

Add the broccoli and corn. (If liquid is low, add more broth.) Cook until the broccoli is done.

Enjoy with crusty bread. Serves two.

Chicken and Lentil Casserole

Sawsan Galal, Sally Webster Inn

Ingredients:

1 cup dry dark lentils	2 tbsp flour
2 ½ cup water	2 cup chicken broth
3 tbsp butter	¾ tsp salt
½ lb mushrooms, sliced	½ tsp pepper
1 medium onion, chopped	1 tbsp chopped dill
1 large carrot, chopped	1 cup chopped cooked chicken
1 medium potato, peeled and chopped	1 cup buttered breadcrumbs (1 cup breadcrumbs with 2-3 tbsp melted butter)

Directions:

Wash lentils. Place in saucepan and cover with water. Bring to a boil, cover and simmer for 20 minutes.

Preheat oven to 350. Melt 2 tbsp butter in sauté pan and add mushrooms. Cook for 2-3 minutes. Remove mushrooms from pan and set aside.

Add remaining butter to pan. Sauté onions, carrots and potato for 3-4 minutes. Stir in flour and blend well. Add broth, salt, pepper and dill. Bring to a boil, stirring constantly. Boil for one minute, then remove from heat. Add the mushrooms and chicken.

Drain lentils. Stir lentils into chicken mixture. Pour into 1 ½ quart casserole dish. Top with buttered breadcrumbs and bake for 30 minutes or until lightly browned and bubbling. Serve hot.

Serves 6

Chicken Breast Stuffed with Spinach, Feta Cheese and Pine Nuts

Sawsan Galal, Sally Webster Inn

Ingredients:
4 skinless, boneless chicken breast halves
1 lb bag frozen chopped spinach, thawed
1 medium onion, minced
3-4 tbsp olive oil
1 cup crumbled Feta cheese
¾ cup shredded Mozzarella cheese
Salt and pepper to taste
¼ tsp nutmeg
¼ cup pine nuts, toasted
¼ cup vegetable oil
1 ½ cup chicken stock

Directions:
In a large sauté pan, sauté onions in olive oil, just until softened. Add thawed spinach and cook until dry. Season with salt, pepper and nutmeg. Allow to cool.

Trim any excess fat off chicken breasts. Place breast with thicker portion towards you. Using a fillet knife or large paring knife, make a slit at the top of the thicker portion. This will create a pocket for the stuffing. Set aside.

Add cheeses to the spinach mix. Stir in the pine nuts.

Using your fingers, stuff the pockets created in the chicken breast. Turn the tail end under and secure with a toothpick or tie with twine. Repeat with remaining breast halves.

Chicken Breast Stuffed with Spinach, Feta Cheese and Pine Nuts
continued

Preheat oven to 350.

Heat the vegetable oil in a large sauté pan. Dry the chicken breasts and season with salt and pepper. Place smooth side down in the oil to sear. Cook for 2-3 minutes on each side. This will seal in the juices and give nice color to the chicken.

Place in a baking dish. Drain excess fat from the pan and deglaze with chicken stock. Pour over chicken and bake in a 350 oven until the internal temperature reads 165 degrees (about 20 minutes). Remove from oven and allow to rest for 10 or so minutes before slicing.

Serves 6-8

GF

Old Coast Guard Station
On Gap Cove (also known as Straitsmouth Cove,) on Marmion Way is the old life-saving station. According to U.S. Coast Guard history, the station was built in 1889 to replace a station built at Davis Neck in 1874. It was originally called Gap Head Station and then, in 1902, became known as Straitsmouth Station. The station remained active until July 1964. It is now a private home.

Pulled Chicken Sandwiches

Sawsan Galal, Sally Webster Inn

Ingredients:

4 skinless, boneless chicken breast halves (about 2 lbs)
Salt and pepper
1 onion, finely chopped
4 cloves garlic, finely chopped
1 1/3 cup barbecue sauce
½ cup apple cider vinegar
Hot pepper sauce
6 Kaiser or French rolls, split
6 oz shredded Monterey Jack cheese (about 1 ½ cups)

Directions:

Season the chicken with salt and pepper and place in a heavy pot with the onion, garlic and just enough water to cover (about 1 ½ cups.)

Add the barbecue sauce, vinegar and a few drops of hot sauce and bring to a boil. Reduce heat and simmer until chicken is cooked through, about 15 minutes. Remove chicken and shred with two forks.

Boil the sauce, skimming occasionally, until reduced by half, about 15 minutes. Season with salt and pepper.

Add the shredded chicken and heat through. Spoon the mixture onto the rolls and top with the cheese.

Chili Con Carne

Nancy Cameron-Gilsey, The Seaward

The perfect winter dish. This is so easy & everyone I make it for asks for the recipe!

Ingredients:
- Olive Oil (or bacon fat)
- 1 large green pepper, chopped
- 2 medium onions, sliced
- 1-1 ½ lbs ground beef
- 2 16 oz cans kidney beans
- 2 16 oz cans stewed tomatoes
- 2 or more tbsp chili powder
- 1 tbsp Worcestershire sauce
- 1 8 oz can tomato sauce
- 2 tsp sugar
- ½ tsp paprika
- ¼ tsp ground cloves
- ¼ tsp garlic powder
- 1 tsp salt (optional)

Directions:
Sauté the pepper and onion in oil or bacon fat.

Add and brown the ground beef. This recipe will work even if you use less than 1 lb ground beef.

Add the beans and tomatoes along with the spices. Stir and simmer until desired thickness.

Test and season to taste.

Cincinnati Chili

Chris Roenker, Seafarer Inn

This is my Dad's recipe. My Dad was raised in Newport, KY, across the river from Cincinnati. He joined the Navy and lived his adult life in San Diego where they don't have chili parlors like they have in Cincy. So, he had to develop his own recipe. We make it at least once a year and it's a special occasion. Thanks, Dad!

Ingredients:
2 lbs lean ground beef
1 lb ground pork
2 medium onions, chopped
2 cans (15 oz) tomato sauce
2 cans (12 oz) tomato paste
10 cups water
3 tsp sugar
3 dashes Worcestershire sauce
2 tbsp red wine vinegar
1 tsp garlic powder

1 tsp black pepper
1 tsp white pepper
½ tsp cayenne pepper
2 tsp cumin
1 tsp marjoram
1 tsp ground allspice
½ tsp ground cloves
5 bay leaves
5 tbsp paprika
1 tbsp cinnamon (reserve)

Directions:
Put beef, pork and onions in a large pot. (Do not brown meat.)
In a blender, blend water, sugar and tomato paste.
In a bowl, mix tomato sauce, vinegar, Worcestershire sauce.
In a separate bowl, combine all dry ingredients (except for the cinnamon.)

Add the water mixture to the pot of meat and combine. Bring to a medium high heat boil. Stir frequently and well until the mixture 'marries,' about 15 minutes.

Add the tomato sauce mixture to the pot. Stir well and lower heat to medium and simmer 15 minutes.

Cincinnati Chili continued

Add the dry ingredients (except cinnamon) to the pot. Stir well, bring to a slight boil, lower heat and simmer with the lid askew on the pot – leaving room for steam to escape. Simmer 2 hours or longer, stirring once in a while. (It won't get really thick, it should be like a sauce.)

½ hour before serving, add cinnamon. Remove bay leaves.

Serve over thin spaghetti with a choice of toppings:
chopped onions, shredded cheddar cheese, kidney beans, oyster crackers.

In Cincinnati, you order by code – which 'way' you want your chili.

Two-**way**: Spaghetti topped with chili (also called "chili spagetts")
Three-**way**: Two way topped with cheese.
Four-way onion: Three way with onions.
Four-way bean: Three way with beans.
Five-way: The works! Spaghetti, chili, beans, onions and cheese.
Coney: A hot dog on a bun covered in chili and cheese.

How to Cook Beef Tenderloin

Debbie Benn, Seven South Street Inn

When it comes to cooking beef tenderloin, less is more. In each steer there are only two tenderloins, running along the spine and non-weight-bearing. This means this is the only cut of meat which does not contain connective tissue, making it tender and flavorful. When we think of filet mignon we need to keep in mind that all that flavor of the meat needs to come through to your guests. Do not overpower the natural flavors by covering the beef with strong spices like rosemary or thyme. Instead create subtle flavors of garlic, salt and pepper to compliment the flavor of the beef. The following recipe will show you how to cook a whole beef tenderloin or filet in easy-to-follow steps.

Ingredients:

1 whole beef tenderloin (any weight, chart below)	Kosher salt
	Cracked pepper corns
Minced garlic - fresh, finely chopped	Rosemary - full sprigs with stems
	Olive oil

Directions:
Preheat oven to 400.

Generously cover your tenderloin with the minced garlic, salt and cracked peppercorns. You may need to gently push the peppercorns into the meat so they stick. Let your meat sit and come to room temperature. Sear all sides before putting in the oven.

Cook in oven and enjoy the aromas.

How to Cook Beef Tenderloin continued

Follow this chart for cooking times and meat temperatures of whole beef tenderloin (filet). Ideally, beef tenderloin should be cooked at 135 to 140 degrees for perfect flavor and temperature.

4 - 5 lbs   35 minutes
5 - 6 lbs   45 minutes
6 - 7 lbs   1 hour
7 - 8 lbs   1 - 1 1/2 hours

Rare	120 - 125 degrees	Center is bright red, outside light red
Medium Rare	130 - 135 degrees	Center is pink, outside light gray / brown
Medium	140 - 145 degrees	Center is pink, outside brown
Medium Well	150 - 155 degrees	Center and outside brown
Well Done	160 + degrees	Darker outside, inside brown

Medium Well and Well done are not recommended for this expensive cut of beef.

Meat resting
Once you pull your meat out of the oven, it's time to let it rest. If you choose to cover your meat for 10-20 minutes, be sure to take it out of the oven 5 degrees below the desired temperature as it will continue to cook out of the oven. Resting will help the juice rehydrate the inside of the meat.

GF

Pot Roast in the Oven
Beth Roenker, Seafarer Inn

Ingredients:
2-4 lbs beef chuck roast (often labeled as "pot roast")
1 can (15 oz) tomato sauce
1 onion
1 package (6 to 8) carrots
Salt and pepper

Directions:
Preheat oven to 350.

Cut the onion into wedges.

In a large casserole dish, pour 1/3 of the tomato sauce in the bottom, place the beef and pour the rest of the tomato sauce over the beef. Sprinkle the onion wedges on and around the beef. Sprinkle with salt and pepper.

Cover and cook in oven for 1 ½ hours.

While the meat is cooking, peel and cut the carrots into chunks.

After 1 ½ hours, turn the meat over and add the carrots to the casserole. (Add a little water if the liquid has been reduced.) Cook for another 1 ½ hours.

Slice the meat and serve with carrots and sauce. Great over baked or mashed potatoes.

Notes:
This recipe is so easy and so foolproof. AND it's delicious. I've tried slow cooker, oven and stove top. This is the very best and now, the only pot roast recipe I ever use.

The leftovers can be shredded and used for tacos the next night.

Swedish Meatballs
Louise Norwood at Rockport Cottage

This is a family favorite handed down by my mother.

Ingredients:
5 lbs ground beef
1 good sized chopped onion
4 or 5 tsp nutmeg
2 separate beaten eggs
½ to ¾ cup of cracker crumbs or bread crumbs
Salt and pepper to taste
Wondra flour
5 or 6 cans of beef consommé (<u>not beef broth</u> as broth will change the desired taste)
Good handful of chopped parsley

Directions:
In large mixing bowl make meatballs in two batches to keep consistency. Mix one half of each ingredient - ground beef, chopped onion, nutmeg, salt & pepper, eggs, parsley and cracker or bread crumbs.

Shape into meatballs and fry in olive oil until brown, reserve the bits of meat in the bottom of the fry pan. Remove the browned meatballs and place in large Dutch oven/kettle. Continue the process until there is no remaining ground beef.

In the fry pan add one half of the consommé stirring up the bits, add Wondra flour to thicken and allow to boil down. Strain the consommé mixture over the meatballs and allow to simmer for a good half hour or better until cooked through. If more liquid is deemed necessary, add another can or two of consommé. Adjust spices to taste i.e. nutmeg, salt and pepper.

Serve over either broad egg noodles or mashed potatoes.

Notes:
I like to use whatever left over crackers I have; place in baggie and crush with rolling pin.

Macaroni and Cheese

Richard Nestel, Lantana House B&B.

Ingredients:

16 oz box macaroni	4 oz stilton cheese crumbled
6 tbsp butter	4 oz Red Leicester cheese, grated
½ cup flour	1 tsp salt
6 oz English cheddar cheese, grated	1 tsp Cajun seasoning
4 oz Irish cheddar cheese, grated	1 tbsp yellow mustard
	1 quart milk

Directions:
Preheat oven to 350. Cook the macaroni 'till done but not soft. Set aside 2 oz of the English cheddar.

Melt the butter over low heat. Stir in the flour 'till you have a smooth paste. Stir in salt, Cajun seasoning and mustard. Cook for 1-2 minutes. Slowly add the milk and bring to a simmer. Simmer for at least 5 minutes till it begins to thicken.

Stir in the cheese (not the 2 oz you have set aside) and remove from the heat.

Drain the cooked macaroni and put in a greased casserole dish. Pour the cheese sauce over the pasta and stir in. Sprinkle the 2 oz of English cheddar over the top.

Bake at 350 for 20 minutes or the top begins to brown.

Notes:
If you like you can add lobster meat to make it a real Rockport dish!

Memere's Easy Baked Macaroni and Cheese
Rosemarie Corundolo, Periwinkle Cottage

No need to make a roux – one pot mac & cheese – kids favorite!

Ingredients:
Elbow macaroni
Butter for greasing pan
6 oz chopped cheddar cheese
Milk
Crushed Ritz crackers

Directions:
To measure – fill casserole dish ½ full of uncooked elbows (will swell when cooked to twice its bulk). Pour out.

Grease dish with butter. Cook elbows until al dente. Drain. Put elbows in dish.

Add 6 oz. chopped cheddar cheese (or more, depending on the size of dish and amount of pasta). Add milk to half way on dish. Put crushed Ritz crackers on top.

Bake about 40 minutes or until milk is absorbed and topping is golden brown.

Beaches
Rockport has 6 beaches: Front Beach, Back Beach, Old Garden Beach, Pebble Beach, Cape Hedge Beach and Long Beach.

Pastierre

Tobey Shepherd, Linden Tree Inn

Our traditional pre-Lent feast!

Ingredients:
- 9 eggs
- 3 cups milk
- 1 ¼ cups sugar
- Pinch of salt
- Ricotta Cheese
- Juice and rind of 1 orange
- 1 pound thick spaghetti, cooked al dente

Directions:
Preheat oven to 350.

Mix eggs, milk, sugar and salt. Blend in ricotta. Add in juice and rind of orange. Stir. Add in spaghetti. Mix well.

Lightly oil baking pans. I use 2 medium-size oval ceramic baking pans. Spread evenly in pans.

Bake at 350 degrees for 45 minutes to an hour. You want it to just start to puff when you take it from the oven as it will still keep cooking once you take it out. Can be eaten warm or cold. When it has cooled, store in the refrigerator.

Notes:
This is typically made for Carnivale, aka Shrove Tuesday, aka Mardi Gras, aka Fat Tuesday. It was a way to use up all your "rich" "fat" ingredients before Lent. In my family we only make it for Carnivale, and no other time. It is so yummy you may want to make it more than once a year, but for me, I keep the tradition, and it makes it that much sweeter when Carnivale rolls around each year!

Roly-Poly Meatloaf

Lynne Norris, Pleasant Street Inn

A fun dinner to make with the kids!

Ingredients:
2/3 cup bread crumbs   ¼ cup chopped onion
1 cup milk   1 tsp salt
2 eggs   ½ tsp sage
1 ½ lb ground beef   dash of pepper

Directions:
Preheat oven to 350.

Combine bread crumbs with milk.

In a separate bowl, beat eggs, then stir into milk mixture.

Add the rest of the ingredients and mix well.

Place in slightly greased muffin tins.

Bake at 350 for 45 minutes.

Serves 8

Stephanie's Favorite Meatloaf Recipe!
Stephanie Smith, Changing Tides Bed & Breakfast

Ingredients:
Meatloaf:
1 onion chopped
3 cloves garlic chopped
2 tsp oil for sautéing onion & garlic
1 lb ground Beef
½ lb ground Pork
½ lb ground Veal
½ tsp thyme
1 tsp salt

2 eggs
3/4 cup crushed Ritz or Saltine crackers
½ cup milk (or yogurt)
2 tsp Worcestershire sauce
2 tsp Dijon mustard
½ tsp pepper
3 or 4 bacon slices

Glaze:
½ cup chili sauce
4 tbsp brown sugar

2 tsp cider vinegar

Directions:
For the glaze: Mix all ingredients in small saucepan; set aside.

For the meatloaf: Preheat oven to 350.

Heat oil in medium skillet. Add onion and garlic; sauté until softened, about 5 minutes. Set aside to cool while preparing remaining ingredients.

Mix eggs with thyme, salt, pepper, mustard, Worcestershire sauce and milk or yogurt. Add egg mixture to meat in large bowl along with crackers and cooked onion and garlic; mix with fork until evenly blended and meat mixture does not stick to bowl.

Stephanie's Favorite Meatloaf Recipe! continued

With wet hands, pat mixture into approximately 9x5-inch loaf shape. Place in foil lined (for easy cleanup) shallow baking pan.

Brush with half the glaze, then arrange bacon slices, crosswise, over loaf, overlapping slightly and tucking only bacon tip ends under loaf.

Bake loaf until bacon is crisp and loaf registers 160 degrees, about 1 hour. Cool at least 20 minutes.

Simmer remaining glaze over medium heat until thickened slightly.

Slice meat loaf and serve with extra glaze.

Notes:
You can use ketchup if you don't have chili sauce.

Cape Ann
Founded by pilgrims in 1623 — and named for England's Queen Anne – the area established villages along the coast, leaving its center a wild woodlands punctuated by granite quarries. Every curve of Cape Ann's rugged coastline offers another scenic beauty: harbors, lighthouses, islands, miles of sandy beaches, quarries, inlets and coves, all so picturesque that artists and moviemakers have flocked here for generations. The four communities that make up Cape Ann; Rockport, Gloucester, Manchester-by-the-Sea and Essex, are home to fishermen and artists, merchants and writers, chefs and farmers who live here year-round.

Aglio e Olio with Clams

Tobey Shepherd, Linden Tree Inn

Ingredients:
4 whole cloves of garlic
Olive oil
½ to 1 pound linguine or thin spaghetti, cooked
Large can of whole small clams or 2 pounds of small raw clams in the shell
Bottle of clam juice

Directions:
Sauté whole garlic cloves in about 1/3 cup of olive oil. Do not let garlic burn. Lower the heat and then carefully add in the clam juice, canned clams and half a cup of water to the pan. Be careful to avoid causing the oil to splatter.

If using raw clams, bring the broth to a boil and add the clams. Cover the pan and allow clams to cook; they are done when they are open. Add salt to taste.

Pour over the cooked spaghetti and serve with a nice salad.

Notes:
You can adjust the amounts of garlic, oil and water, clam juice and clams according to how many people you want to feed.

Sea Scallops with Roasted Red Pepper Cream
Mike Barnhard, The Yankee Clipper Inn

Ingredients:

6 tbsp butter, divided	½ cup light cream
1 medium onion, finely chopped	2 tsp lemon juice
2 garlic cloves, minced	1 tbsp EVOO
2 or 3 roasted red peppers, peeled, chopped, seeded and pureed	3 lb scallops
	Chopped parsley (optional)
	Lemon wedges (optional)
1 tsp salt and pepper	

Directions:
Heat 4 tbsp butter in a pan over medium heat. Add onion, garlic, bell pepper and salt and pepper. Sauté until the onion is soft.

Add cream and lemon juice. Reduce and thicken slightly. Puree'.

Melt 2 tbsp butter and EVOO on high heat. Sear scallops 30 seconds per side. Turn once.

Serve with sauce. Garnish with lemon wedges and parsley.

Crab Cakes with Lemon Tarragon Cream

Mike Barnhard, The Yankee Clipper Inn

Ingredients:
2 ½ lb crab, coarsely chopped
3 cups panko bread crumbs
3 eggs, beaten
¾ cup mayonnaise
¾ cup diced celery
¾ cup diced Vidalia onion
Canola oil for frying

Directions:
With your hands, blend 1 cup panko crumbs with crab and add eggs, mayo, celery and onion. Form into hockey puck-sized patties.

Press patties into remaining panko crumbs. Rest on wax paper. (May be made to this point a day ahead and refrigerated.)

Heat oil over medium-high heat. Fry in batches without crowding until crisp and brown, turning once. Keep warm on a cookie sheet in a 200 degree oven.

Cream Sauce:
8 tbsp butter
1 cup minced shallot
2 cup dry white wine
1 1/3 cup heavy cream
¼ cup minced tarragon 4 tbsp Pernod or other anise-flavored liqueur
Zest of 1 lemon

Directions:
Melt butter, add shallots and cook for 3 minutes.
Add wine and boil to reduce by ½. Add cream, tarragon, Pernod, and simmer until sauce clings to the back of a spoon.

Serve crab cakes topped with sauce and sprinkled with lemon zest.

Baked Haddock

Nancy Cameron-Gilsey, The Seaward

This is a classic recipe from the kitchen of Seaward Inn. It can be found in the Seaward Inn's cookbook, "Pierre Tells All - The Cook's Book"

Ingredients:
1 stick butter   1 pound haddock fillets

Crumb mix:
½ stick butter   1 tbsp chopped parsley
½ tsp onion powder   dash Worcestershire sauce
¼ tsp garlic powder   25 to 30 Ritz crackers
½ tsp Lawry's seasoning

Directions:
Preheat oven to 350.

Melt 1 stick of butter. Cut haddock into serving portions.

Dip fish in butter and then in seasoned crumb mixture (below). Place fish in buttered 9x12 baking dish. Bake at 350 degrees for 20 to 25 minutes or until fish flakes. Serves 4.

Seasoned Crumbs:
Melt ½ stick butter and add the seasonings and Worcestershire sauce. Crush the Ritz crackers and add to the butter mixture.

Notes:
The seasoned crumb mix is great for Lobster pie and baked shrimp, as well.

Boiled Lobster

Chris & Beth Roenker, Seafarer Inn

Ingredients:
1 ¼ - 1 ½ pound lobsters   lemon
salted water   butter

Directions:
Fill a large stockpot about half full of water. Add 2 or 3 tbsp of salt and bring to a boil.

When the water has come to a rolling boil, plunge the lobsters headfirst into the pot. Clamp the lid back on tightly and return the water to a boil over high heat. Reduce the heat to medium and cook the lobsters for 12 to 18 minutes (hard-shell lobsters will take the longer time), until the shells turn bright red and the tail meat is firm and opaque when checked.

Serve with lemon wedges and melted butter.

How to eat a boiled lobster:

- Twist off the lobster claws.
- Crack each lobster claw and knuckle with a lobster cracker.
- Separate the lobster tail from the body.
- Crack the flippers off the end of the tail.
- Push the tail meat out of the tail in one piece.
- Remove the black vein that runs the length of the tail.
- Enjoy the meat from the legs by biting down and squeezing the meat out with your teeth.
- There is also meat in the lobster's tail flippers.
- Try the tomalley (the green substance in the body.) Some people consider this a delicacy.

Salads & Sides

The Seafarer Inn

The Seafarer Inn is a casual, comfortable home by the sea. An antique Dutch Colonial directly across the street from historic Straitsmouth Cove, the house has 6 guest rooms, each with an ocean view and a private bathroom.

The Seafarer Inn has a long history as a place to stay to get away from it all when visiting Rockport. Built in 1890, the Seafarer Inn was part of the Straitsmouth Inn and was known as "Old Cottage." We took over the house in 2013 and have worked hard to continue the proud tradition of hospitality long known to the Seafarer.

A stay at the Seafarer comes with a complimentary, buffet-style breakfast each morning featuring both hot and cold offerings. Each day we offer both an egg dish and a sweet entrée along with breakfast meats and breads. Our house specialty is the Seafarer Yogurt Parfait Bar. Help yourself to a variety of yogurt flavors and top your parfait with fresh fruit and any of a number of toppings such as coconut, chopped walnuts, chocolate chips or sunflower seeds.

Our guests love to relax on the front porch or by the koi pond while they watch the boats cruise by and breathe in the fresh sea air. We work to make our home comfortable so that our guests feel as though they are visiting the family beach house. The Seafarer is a mile out of town on a quiet, residential street. Our main traffic is made up of morning joggers and dog walkers.

Come visit the Seafarer for a relaxing, comfortable stay by the sea.

Seafarer Inn...*your home by the sea*
50 Marmion Way, Rockport, Massachusetts 01966
978-546-6248
info@seafarer-inn.com
www.seafarer-inn.com

Poppie's Potato Salad

Beth Roenker, Seafarer Inn

My Dad, known to the grandkids as "Poppie," was very particular that the potatoes be cut into small pieces. In our family, it just isn't a summer party without Poppie's potato salad. It's still my favorite potato salad recipe!

Ingredients:

3 lbs red skinned potatoes	2 tbsp mustard
4 stalks celery	2 tbsp apple cider vinegar
6 or 8 green onions	½ tsp celery seed
1 cup mayonnaise	Salt and pepper to taste

Directions:
Clean potatoes and cut into small pieces.

Boil potatoes until done. Cool.

Chop celery and green onions and mix into potatoes.

Mix together mayonnaise, mustard, vinegar, celery seed and salt and pepper.

Gently mix sauce into potato mixture.

GF

Cucumber Salad

Beth Roenker, Seafarer Inn

I love this salad because it is easy, foolproof and always a favorite. Plus, it travels well. I make it for almost every summer party I go to or host!

Ingredients:
- 3 cucumbers, peeled, thinly sliced
- 1 medium onion, thinly sliced
- ½ cup seasoned rice vinegar
- ½ tsp salt
- Freshly ground pepper

Directions:
Combine and mix all ingredients in a large bowl.

Cover and refrigerate for at least 2 hours or overnight.

Drain before serving. May be served chilled or at room temperature.

GF VG

The Granite Keystone Bridge

The Keystone Bridge is an historic bridge that carries Granite Street (Massachusetts Route 127) over the former railroad that transported granite from Pigeon Hill to Granite Pier in Rockport, Massachusetts. The bridge arch was built in 1872 in eleven weeks. Its single arch spans 65 feet (20 m) and is 32 feet (9.8 m) wide. The bridge was added to the National Register of Historic Places in 1981.

Grilled Caesar Salad

Chris & Beth Roenker, Seafarer Inn

We love this as a starter when we gather around the grill for a summer dinner. It doesn't need dressing, but some prefer it with a dressing, so I always offer one, whether homemade or store-bought.

Ingredients:
Romain Hearts
Olive oil for brushing
Garlic powder or clove
Freshly ground black pepper
Grated parmesan cheese
Caesar salad dressing
Toasted French bread or croutons

Directions:
Cut the Romain hearts lengthwise. Brush the cut side with oil and sprinkle with garlic powder (or rub with garlic clove.)

When your grill is hot, grill the lettuce, cut side down for 10 to 30 seconds until just starting to char.

Serve the grilled lettuce on individual plates, sprinkled with cheese. Offer dressing and toast on the side.

Holiday Vegetable Mix

Beth Roenker, Seafarer Inn

I was inspired to come up with a gluten free, vegan side dish for Thanksgiving because the guest list included family with various food allergies. I wanted something everyone could enjoy.

Ingredients:
- Oil for sautéing
- 1 onion, chopped
- 2 large carrots, peeled and chopped
- 2 celery stalks, chopped
- 1 small head of cauliflower, chopped small
- 1 cup chopped mushrooms
- Kosher salt
- Freshly ground pepper
- ¼ cup chopped fresh parsley
- 2 tbsp chopped fresh rosemary
- 1 tbsp chopped fresh sage
- 1 cup vegetable broth

Directions:
In a large skillet, over medium heat, heat oil. Add onion, carrot and celery and sauté until soft, about 7 or 8 minutes.

Add cauliflower and season with salt and pepper. Cook until tender, 8-10 minutes.

Add mushrooms and herbs and combine. Add vegetable broth and cover. Simmer until totally tender and liquid is absorbed, about 15 or 20 minutes.

Notes:
This dish can be made a day ahead which is GREAT for a holiday dinner. It travels well and heats easily stovetop, in the oven or in the microwave. And it tastes just like stuffing!!

GF VG

Cantaloupe and Cucumber Salad

Sawsan Galal, Sally Webster Inn

Ingredients:
½ cup Greek style yogurt
2 tbsp lime juice
2 tbsp honey
¼ cup cold water
3 stalks celery, chopped
1 cantaloupe cut into bite size pieces
1 cucumber peeled and cut into bite size pieces
½ cup mint, chopped
Toasted almonds

Directions:
In a large bowl, whisk together yogurt, lime juice, water and honey.

Add the cantaloupe, cucumber, celery and mint and mix.

Sprinkle with toasted almonds.

GF

First Congregational Church Steeple, "Old Sloop"
On Sept. 8, 1814, during the War of 1812, the British frigate Nymph launched a barge to invade Sandy Bay. When the meetinghouse bell of the Congregational Church sounded the alarm, the crew fired at the bell to silence it. The shot failed to damage the steeple and the cannon went through the bottom of the barge, sinking it. The cannon is nearby on the lawn and the church still has the cannonball. Look up at the steeple to see a replica cannonball!

Roasted Beet Salad with Citrus Dressing

Helene Duffy, The Beech Tree B&B

Even if you think you hate beets, I encourage you to try this! I never eat beets but when my Quebecoise friend, Cynthia Borghesani, introduced my taste buds to this nutritional powerhouse, I was won over.

Ingredients:
4 med beets, red and yellow (sweeter)
1/3 cup chopped walnuts or halved pecans
3 tbsp maple syrup
½ cup frozen orange juice concentrate
¼ cup balsamic vinegar (I used white balsamic)
½ cup EVOO
1 10 oz pk baby salad greens
2 oz goat cheese (I use the pre-crumbled)

Directions:
Roast the beets in a 400 degree oven for 1 hour. Cool, peel and cut into pieces (size can be to your liking.)

Heat nuts in skillet until fragrant. Add maple syrup to coat and cook gently. Watch carefully to pull off heat quickly. Separate from sticking together and cool.

Whisk OJ, vinegar and EVOO together.

Toss salad greens with beets, goat cheese and nuts. Drizzle with dressing and toss again. Makes 4-6 servings

Notes:
Variations include marinating the beets in the dressing or using prepared beets. I do not. You can use white or dark balsamic vinegar. The OJ concentrate is heartier and makes a thicker dressing.

Corn Pudding

Lynne Norris, Pleasant Street Inn

Ingredients:
1 8 oz can creamed corn
1 8 oz can whole kernel corn, drained
½ pint sour cream
1 8 oz box of Jiffy corn muffin mix
2 eggs, slightly beaten
1 stick melted butter (8 tbsp)
¾ cup grated Swiss cheese

Directions:
Preheat oven to 350. Combine all ingredients except the cheese.

Pour into 1 ¾ qt greased baking dish or a 9x9 pan.

Bake for 35 minutes.

Remove from oven and sprinkle Swiss cheese on top.

Bake an additional 10 minutes.

Notes:
This is a great side dish for Thanksgiving dinner!

Stephanie's Boston Baked Beans
Stephanie Smith, Changing Tides Bed & Breakfast

Ingredients:
2 16 oz packages dried navy beans
4 tsp salt
¾ cup dark molasses
½ cup packed dark brown sugar
1 tbsp dry mustard
1 tsp pepper
1 large onion
4-6 whole cloves
1 meaty ham bone or salt pork
Pinch baking soda

Directions:
Prepare beans: Rinse well and discard any stones or shriveled beans. Soak beans in water in a 5 quart Dutch oven overnight. (Use about 3 cups of water to 1 cup of beans.)

Bring mixture to a boil, add salt and a pinch of baking soda, reduce heat, cover and simmer for an hour.

Preheat oven to 250.

Stir in molasses and next 3 ingredients.

Stud the onion with the cloves; tuck onion & ham bone (or salt pork) into the beans.

Cover and bake in a 250 oven for about 7-10 hours; check & stir about once an hour.

Add more water to keep beans moist but not too wet OR remove lid to thicken mixture through evaporation; it all depends on your preference for thick or runny.

Mixed Grain Salad with Dried Fruit

Sawsan Galal, Sally Webster Inn

Ingredients:
- ½ cup wild rice
- ½ cup brown rice
- ½ cup Spelt grain (wheat berries or pearl barley may also be used)
- 4 cups water
- 1 tsp salt
- ¾ cup dried cranberries
- ¼ cup chopped dried apricots
- ¼ cup raisins (optional)
- ½ cup favorite chopped nuts
- Herbs of choice to taste (parsley, dill, chopped chives or scallions)
- ½ cup rice wine vinegar
- 2 tbsp olive oil
- 1 tsp garlic powder
- Salt to taste
- 2 tbsp chopped fresh tarragon, or 1 tbsp dried tarragon

Directions:
Bring 2 cups of water to a boil. Add half of salt. Drop in wild rice and allow to boil until soft to the bite (around 10-15 minutes.) Drain and reserve for later use.

Bring remaining water to boil and drop in brown rice and Spelt. Add remaining amount of salt. Bring to a boil and reduce until water is absorbed and grains are tender, (around 40 minutes.) If more water is needed, add ¼ cup of water at a time, allowing for full absorption before adding more water. Remove from heat and allow to cool slightly.

In a separate small bowl, mix olive oil, vinegar, garlic powder, tarragon and salt. Add to rice mixture and toss to coat. Add remaining ingredients and adjust seasonings.

Yields 6-8 servings

GF VG

Patatas Bravas (Spicy Spanish Potatoes)
Sawsan Galal, Sally Webster Inn

Ingredients:
2 lbs potatoes, quartered, skin on (red skin or golden)
1 tbsp olive oil
Salt and pepper to taste
1 can chopped tomatoes, liquid drained
1 tbsp tomato puree
3 cloves garlic
½ a white onion
½ tsp smoked paprika
½ tsp cayenne pepper*
2 tsp olive oil, for cooking.

Directions:
Preheat the oven to 400. Place the quartered potatoes in a pot of boiling water for 5 minutes. Drain and allow to steam dry in the strainer for a couple of minutes.

Arrange the partially cooked potatoes in a large roasting tray and toss with the olive oil, salt and pepper so that each quarter is evenly coated. Cook for 30-35 minutes, tossing once during the cooking process.

Put all of the ingredients for the bravas sauce in a food processor except for the olive oil. Blend until you have a smooth sauce. Heat the olive oil in a frying pan and add sauce to oil and cook for 5 minutes on a medium to high heat to reduce slightly.

Serve the potatoes immediately, topped with the warm sauce. Serve some mayonnaise and fresh parsley on the side.

Notes:
*Adjust the cayenne pepper depending on how spicy you want the sauce. ½ tsp will create a medium spiced sauce; reduce or increase the amount as you wish.

GF VG

Cous Cous
Tobey Shepherd, Linden Tree Inn

Ingredients:
1 ½ cups plain cous cous
2 cups chicken broth, vegetable broth or water
1 garlic clove, thinly sliced
Salt and pepper to taste
1 tbsp of olive oil
½ tsp Herbs de Provence
1 tsp oregano
2 tbsp grated Romano or parmesan cheese
Handful of pine nuts lightly toasted (optional)

Directions:
Bring all ingredients but the cous cous to a boil and simmer for 2 minutes (to let the garlic cook some.)

Add cous cous and stir well. Cover and turn off burner. Let stand for 5 minutes. Fluff with a fork and serve.

Notes:
You can experiment with the amounts and types of herbs to create a taste you like.

Hannah Jumper

For about 150 years Rockport was a dry town. This dates back to 1856 when Hannah Jumper, frustrated by the excessive consumption of alcohol by the townsmen, led her hatchet brigade of women through Dock Square smashing barrels and bottles of booze. Her hatchet can be seen at the Sandy Bay historical building. Her house, built in 1740 and recently renovated, is located at 35 Mount Pleasant Street. Her grave can be found in the Old First Parish Burying Ground on Beach Street.

In 2006 the town voted to allow alcohol to be served in restaurants with the consumption of food. Shortly after, that restriction was relaxed so that now, visitors can enjoy a cocktail, wine or beer without ordering food at any of several pubs and bars in town. In 2019, a local market was permitted, for the first time in over 150 years, to sell beer and wine to consumers! Rockport has buried the hatchet!

Desserts

The Emerson Inn

The Emerson Inn is a classic Massachusetts oceanfront hotel, perfectly situated between panoramic Halibut Point and charming Bearskin Neck, in Rockport. With over 150 years of history, our Rockport hotel has welcomed travelers from near and far seeking rest and relaxation on scenic Pigeon Cove in a relaxing, natural oceanfront setting. Beautifully restored to offer our guests modern amenities and conveniences while maintaining the charm & grace of yesteryear, the Inn is a perfect getaway for North Shore family vacations, romantic getaways on Cape Ann, or solo travelers seeking rest & respite along the ruggedly beautiful Cape Ann coastline.

Pigeon Cove Tavern, our on-site restaurant, perfectly encapsulates quintessential New England comfort food with sophistication and intuition. Characterized by our commitment to New England fare done right, such as chowder, lobster rolls and other local favorites, the tavern is the perfect meeting place for any occasion. Whether enjoying appetizers and a couple drinks after a day on the town, toasting to a special date with a romantic candlelit dinner or just savoring that perfect lobster roll, at Pigeon Cove Tavern we celebrate simplicity with our unique take on sophisticated comfort food.

The Emerson Inn
1 Cathedral Ave Rockport, Massachusetts 01966
978-546-6321
info@emersoninnbythesea.com
www.theemersoninn.com

Crème Brulee'
The Emerson Inn

Ingredients:
6 egg yolks
1 quart cream
½ cup sugar
1 tsp vanilla

Directions:
Preheat oven to 300.

Heat cream in a pot, bring to a boil then reduce heat.

In a mixing bowl, whisk egg yolks, sugar and vanilla, until yolks are thick and have a pale yellow color.

Whisk in hot cream 1 ladle at time until all of the cream is incorporated.

Pass the mix through a fine chinois. Place ceramic dishes in a 2 inch hotel pan and pour in cream mixture.

Use a blow torch to get rid of any bubbles on the surface. Carefully pour hot water into the hotel pan and tightly cover with foil.

Bake in the oven at 300 degrees with low fan, for 45-50 minutes.

GF

Chocolate Mousse
The Emerson Inn

Ingredients:
1 quart cream
4 oz powdered sugar
1 tsp vanilla 1 quart chopped dark chocolate
2 tbsp granulated sugar
10 egg whites
1 oz whiskey (optional)

Directions:
Put cream, powdered sugar and vanilla in a stand mixer with the whisk attachment; whisk until you have whipped cream with stiff peaks. Keep cool.

Place chopped chocolate in a metal bowl and melt it over a pot of boiling water.

In a clean mixing bowl, add egg whites and granulated sugar; mix on medium speed. When foamy, add whiskey and increase speed to high.

When chocolate is fully melted, pour it into the egg whites while the mixer is running. Once all the chocolate is in the egg whites, pour all of the mix into a larger mixing bowl and fold in the whipped cream one third at a time. Cool and serve chilled.

GF

Debbie's Kahlua Cake

Rosemarie Cerundolo, Periwinkle Cottage

A decadent cake that makes any party fancy. Try different liquors too!

Ingredients:
- 18 ½ oz box Devil's Food w/pudding cake mix
- 4 oz package instant chocolate pudding
- 4 eggs, beaten
- ½ cup vegetable oil
- 1 cup sour cream (or plain yogurt)
- 1 ½ cups total (your choice of): Coffee, Kahlua, Frangelico, Bailey's
- Confectioner's sugar for garnish

Preheat oven to 350. Grease Bundt pan.

Mix all ingredients above and pour into pan and bake 45-50 minutes (and test with toothpick).

When cool, top with confectioner's sugar.

Serve with ice cream and caramel sauce or fresh strawberries and whipped cream.

Crème Brulee'

Sawsan Galal, Sally Webster Inn

Ingredients:

1 quart heavy cream	1 cup sugar, divided
1 vanilla bean, split and scraped	6 large egg yolks
or 1 ½ tsp vanilla extract	2 quarts hot water

Directions

Preheat the oven to 325 degrees.
Place the cream, vanilla bean and its pulp into a medium saucepan set over medium-high heat and bring to a boil. Remove from the heat, cover and allow to sit for 15 minutes. Remove the vanilla bean and reserve for another use. If using vanilla extract, heat cream to a simmer then add extract.

In a medium bowl, whisk together ½ cup sugar and the egg yolks until well blended and it just starts to lighten in color. Add the cream a little at a time, stirring continually.

Pour the liquid into 6 (7 or 8-ounce) ramekins. Place the ramekins into a large cake pan or roasting pan. Pour enough hot water into the pan to come halfway up the sides of the ramekins. Bake just until the Crème Brulee' is set but still trembling in the center, approximately 40-45 minutes.

Remove the ramekins from the roasting pan and refrigerate for at least 2 hours and up to 3 days.

Crème Brulee' continued

Remove the Crème Brulee' from the refrigerator for at least 30 minutes prior to browning the sugar on top.

Divide the remaining ½ cup sugar equally among the 6 dishes and spread evenly on top.

Using a torch, melt the sugar and form a crispy top. Allow the Crème Brulee' to sit for at least 5 minutes before serving.

***Propane gas torches are highly flammable and should be kept away from heat, open flame and prolonged exposure to sunlight. They should be used only in well-ventilated areas. Follow torch manufacturer's instructions for use.

GF

Straitsmouth Island
Off Gap Head Road and Straitsmouth Cove is Straitsmouth Island which was first sighted in 1614 by Captain John Smith. He also spotted nearby Thacher and Milk Islands and named all three the Turks' Heads. Built in 1834, the island's first lighthouse was 19 feet tall. The original tower was replaced by a second tower in 1896. It was automated in 1967 and is still in operation. Its construction was spurred by the increasing number of ships sailing to Pigeon Cove for cargoes of stone from Rockport's burgeoning granite industry. Marking the entrance to Rockport Harbor, the light also warned mariners of the Dry Salvages reef and Avery's Ledge.

Strawberry Rhubarb Crisp
The Emerson Inn

Ingredients:
1 lb butter
1 lb frozen rhubarb
1 tbsp grated ginger
1 pint brown sugar
1 pint granulated sugar
1 oz lemon juice
1 tsp salt
1 quart washed sliced strawberries

Crumble Topping:
½ lb softened butter
1 cup brown sugar
1 cup granulated sugar
2 cups all-purpose flour
2 cups oats
1 tsp salt
1 tbsp cinnamon

Directions:
Preheat oven to 325. In a large rondeau or sauce pan, heat butter. When lightly brown and foaming, add rhubarb and stir.

When rhubarb is soft and cooked down add ginger, brown sugar, granulated sugar and salt. Let cook until thick; taste and adjust if necessary. Add cut strawberries and lemon juice and let sit for 5 minutes. Pour mix into a bowl to cool.

Pour into a baking dish, top with crumble mix and bake at 325 for approximately 20 minutes until it is golden brown and hot in the center.

Crumble Directions:
Combine softened butter and both sugars in a stand mixer with paddle attachment and mix until it develops a creamy texture. Add remaining ingredients and stir on low until it has a crumbly texture.

Apple Crisp
The Emerson Inn

Ingredients:
Filling:
5 lb Granny Smith apples peeled & sliced
5 lb Honey Crisp apples peeled & sliced
1 cup sugar

Topping:
½ lb butter
1 cup brown sugar
½ cup flour
½ cup oats

1 tsp salt
1 cup brown sugar
1 lb butter
2 cups dried or fresh cranberries
1 oz lemon juice

1 tsp cinnamon
1 tsp nutmeg
1 tsp salt

Directions:
Preheat oven to 325.
Topping:
In stand mixer add butter and sugar; mix until creamy. Add flour, oats and seasoning mix until mixture is crumbled. Pour on sheet pan and bake for 15 minutes. Break up mixture and re-bake 15 minutes.

Filling:
Lower oven to 300. In a large rondeau or sauce pan, heat butter. When lightly brown and foaming, add the apples and stir. When apples are soft and cooked down, add brown sugar, granulated sugar and salt. Let cook until thick; taste and adjust if necessary.

Add cranberries and lemon juice and let sit for 5 minutes. Pour mix into bowl to cool. Pour filling mixture into baking dish, bake at 300 for 20 minutes. Add crumb topping, cook for additional 10 minutes or until golden brown.

Apple Cake
Sawsan Galal, Sally Webster Inn

Ingredients:
3/4 cup all-purpose flour
3/4 tsp baking powder
Pinch of salt
2 large eggs
3 tbsp dark rum or other flavoring (concentrated juice can be used)
3/4 cup sugar
½ tsp pure vanilla extract
1 stick unsalted butter, melted and cooled
4 large apples (if you can, choose 4 different kinds) cored and diced.

Directions:
Center a rack in the oven and preheat the oven to 350. Generously butter an 8-inch springform pan and put it on a baking sheet lined with a silicone baking mat or parchment paper and put the springform on it.

Whisk the flour, baking powder and salt together in small bowl.

In a medium bowl, beat the eggs with a whisk until they're foamy. Pour in the sugar and whisk for a minute or so to blend. Whisk in the rum and vanilla.

Whisk in half the flour mixture and when it is incorporated, add half the melted butter followed by the rest of the flour and the remaining butter, mixing gently after each addition so that you have a smooth, rather thick batter.

Switch to a rubber spatula and fold in the apples, turning the fruit so that it's coated with batter. Scrape the mix into the pan and poke it around a little with the spatula so that it's even.

Apple Cake continued

Slide the pan into the oven and bake for 50-60 minutes or until the top of the cake is golden brown and a knife inserted deep into the center comes out clean; the cake may pull away from the sides of the pan. Transfer to a cooling rack and let rest for 5 minutes.

Allow the cake to cool until it is just slightly warm or at room temperature.

If you want to remove the cake from the bottom of the springform pan, wait until the cake is almost cooled, then run a long spatula between the cake and the pan, cover the top of the cake with a piece of parchment or wax paper and invert it onto a rack. Carefully remove the bottom of the pan and turn the cake over onto a serving dish.

Harvest Fest
On the third Saturday in October, New England food producers gather on T-Wharf and in Harvey park to celebrate the best of local food with fresh lobster, chowder, pastries, grass-fed beef, wood-fired pizza, small-batch jams, locally-grown produce and more. You will also find craft beers produced in Massachusetts and Rockport's own Twin Lights tonic, soda crafted from the 120-year-old company's original recipes. Cooking demonstrations take place throughout the day demonstrating the riches of harvest in New England. Harvest Fest features plenty of live bluegrass, jazz, folk, indie rock, cooking demos, a farm expo and plenty of activities for families. www.rockportexchange.com

Peach Oat Crisp

Lynne Norris, Pleasant Street Inn

Ingredients:
2 cans (15 oz each) yellow cling peaches, drained
½ cup flour
1/3 cup firmly packed brown sugar
1/3 cup old fashioned oats
¼ tsp cinnamon
1/3 cup chopped walnuts
1/3 cup melted butter

Directions:
Preheat oven to 425.

Place drained fruit in an 8x8 baking dish.

Combine flour, sugar, oats, cinnamon and walnuts.

Mix in butter until crumbly and sprinkle evenly over the fruit.

Bake at 425 for 15-20 minutes until topping is golden.

Notes:
Can be a breakfast dish or a dessert with ice cream or whipped cream!

Chocolate Pie
Louise Norwood, Rockport Cottages

Ingredients:
6 milk chocolate bars with almonds (such as Hershey's)
18 marshmallows
½ cup milk
Dash of salt
½ pint of whipped cream
Graham cracker crust

Directions:
In the top of a double boiler, melt bars and marshmallows with milk. Add salt. Remove from heat and cool.

Add whipped cream. Fold in until all are mixed. Pour into graham cracker crust. Freeze 2 ½ hours. Garnish with whipped cream.

Peanut Butter Pie
Louise Norwood, Rockport Cottages

Ingredients:
8 oz cream cheese softened
14 oz can sweetened condensed milk
¾ cup creamy peanut butter
1 tbsp lemon juice
1 tsp vanilla
4 oz Cool Whip (or whipped cream)
Chocolate syrup
Chocolate readymade crust (or regular pie crust)

Directions:
Beat cream cheese until fluffy; beat in sweetened condensed milk and peanut butter until smooth. Stir in lemon juice and vanilla.

Fold in whipped cream or Cool Whip. Turn into crust. Drizzle chocolate syrup over pie and refrigerate until set. Enjoy!

Baklava
Sawsan Galal, Sally Webster Inn

Ingredients:
1 lb phyllo, thawed
½ lb unsalted butter
16 oz finely chopped walnuts
1 tbsp ground cinnamon
¼ cup sugar

For syrup:
2 cups sugar
1 cup water
2 tsp lemon juice
1 tsp vanilla

Directions:
Preheat oven to 350.

Make the syrup:
In a small saucepan, mix water and sugar. Bring to a boil and add lemon juice. Simmer for about 10 minutes or until it coats the back of a metal spoon. Allow to cool completely before adding the vanilla extract.

Assemble the baklava:
Mix nuts, ¼ cup of sugar and cinnamon in a small bowl. Brush the bottom and sides of a 13x9-inch baking pan with melted butter.

Cut phyllo sheets to fit the pan. Stack sheets and cover with clear plastic wrap and slightly damp cloth. Lay out 1 cut sheet of phyllo at the bottom of the pan and brush evenly with butter. Continue layering with butter and phyllo until you have laid down 8 sheets.

Spread the chopped nut mixture over the eighth layer and spread evenly. Repeat the process used to cover the bottom of the pan with another eight sheets. Be very careful not to dry out the remaining dough while layering.

Baklava continued

With a serrated knife, cut through the phyllo to make square or diamond shaped pieces.

Bake in a 350 oven until it turns a light golden brown. Depending on your oven, it may take from 20 to 25 minutes.

Remove from the oven and drench in the cooled syrup. It is important that the syrup is cold when the baklava comes out of the oven, otherwise, it will result in a soggy pastry.

Allow to cool before serving. This will give the pastry time to absorb the syrup.

Old Stone Fort
At the end of Bearskin Neck is the site of a fort erected by public subscription as a protection against British warships during the War of 1812. The fort was captured in a sneak attack and dismantled by the frigate Nymph. With ammunition gone and all nine sea fencibles taken prisoner, the townsmen hurled rocks, using their stockings as slings.

"Sea Fencible" is a term taken from the British. In June 1813 the US Senate Naval Affairs Committee reported "there are seafaring men, who from their hardihood and habits of life, might be very useful in the defense of the seaboard, particularly in the management of the great guns..." On July 26, 1813, during the War of 1812 with the United Kingdom, the United States Congress passed "An act to authorize the raising [of] a Corps of Sea Fencibles ... not to exceed one year [service] and not to exceed ten companies who may be employed for the defense of the ports and harbors of the United States..."

Martha's Pecan Pie

Louise Norwood, Rockport Cottages

I still have the handwritten recipe given to me by our beloved cousin Martha Jane Coulbourn.

Ingredients:
- ½ cup pecan halves
- 1 cup sugar
- 1 cup dark corn syrup
- 3 eggs beaten lightly
- 1 tbsp melted butter
- 1 tsp vanilla (scant)
- pie crust (readymade or homemade)

Directions:
Preheat oven to 375.

Mix sugar, butter, syrup and vanilla and add to beaten eggs.

Place pecans in pattern on bottom crust and pour mixture over pecans.

Bake at 375 for 40 minutes.

Chocolate Streusel Bars

Richard Nestel, Lantana House B&B

Ingredients:
1 ¾ cups all-purpose flour
1 ½ cups powdered sugar
½ cup unsweetened cocoa powder
1 cup cold butter (2 sticks)
1 8 oz pkg cream cheese
1 14 oz can sweetened condensed milk
1 egg, beaten
2 tsp vanilla

Directions:
Preheat oven to 350.

In a bowl combine flour, sugar and cocoa. Cut in butter with a pastry blender until crumbly.

<u>Set aside 2 cups of the mixture</u>. Press the remainder into a 13x9 baking pan. Bake for 15 minutes.

In a bowl, beat cream cheese 'till fluffy. Beat in condensed milk 'till creamy. Add the egg and vanilla. Mix well. Pour over the pre-baked crust.

Sprinkle the remaining 2 cups of mixture over filling.

Bake for 20 minutes or until it bubbles.

Cool and then chill. Cut into bars and serve.

Lemon Bars
Richard Nestel, Lantana House B&B

Ingredients:
1 cup butter (2 sticks)
¼ tsp salt
½ cup powdered sugar
2 ¼ cup all-purpose flour, divided

2 cups granulated sugar
4 eggs beaten
6 tbsp lemon juice
Powdered sugar for dusting

Directions:
Preheat oven to 350.

In a bowl combine the butter, salt, powdered sugar and 2 cups flour. Mix well.

Press into a 9x13 baking pan. Bake 15-20 minutes or until golden brown. Cool.

In a bowl combine ¼ cup flour and the granulated sugar. Stir in the eggs and lemon juice.

Pour over the cooled crust.

Bake for 25 minutes or until a toothpick comes out clean.

Cool then sift powdered sugar over the top. Cut and serve.

Gluten Free Oatmeal-Apple Cookies

Debbie Benn, Seven South Street Inn

Ingredients:

1 apple (I like Honey Crisp)	5 tbsp softened butter
2 cups GF rolled oats	¼ cup brown sugar
1 ½ cups almond flour	1 tsp vanilla
1/2 tsp baking powder	½ cup sliced almonds
¼ tsp salt	

Directions:
Preheat oven to 350. Line 2 cookie sheets with parchment.

Coarsely grate the apple.

In a medium bowl, combine the oats, almond flour, baking powder and salt.

In a large bowl, using a hand mixer beat the grated apple with butter, brown sugar and vanilla. Add dry ingredients and beat until well combined (dough will be somewhat crumbly)

With a small cookie scoop or tbsp, scoop and roll dough into balls and place on lined cookie sheets, spacing 2 inches apart.

Top each cookie with sliced almonds and press to flatten for crisp cookies.

Bake 15 minutes, switching racks halfway through. Cool cookies on wire racks. Oh, so good! Enjoy!

Makes 18 Cookies

Notes:
Adapted from Clean Eating Magazine

GF

Rhubarb Crumb Bars
Stephanie Smith, Changing Tides Bed & Breakfast

Ingredients:
¾ cup all-purpose flour
½ cup whole spelt (or whole wheat pastry) flour
¼ tsp salt
1 stick unsalted butter, plus 1 additional tbsp, cut into ½ inch chunks and softened to cool room temperature
1/3 cup sugar
¼ cup oats
¼ cup pecans, finely chopped
2 tbsp light (or dark) brown sugar
A large pinch of flaky salt (such as Maldon or fleur de sel)
1 ¼ cup rhubarb jam (see recipe in "Jams, Jellies & Sauces" chapter)

Directions:
Position a rack in the center of the oven and preheat to 375. Line an 8×8 square pan with two crisscrossing slings of parchment paper (or heavy-duty aluminum foil), leaving a 1" overhang on each side.

In the bowl of a stand mixer fitted with the paddle attachment, combine the flours, sugar and salt. Mix on low to combine, then, with the mixer running, add 8 tbsp of the butter 1 piece at a time. Mix for a minute or two until the crust mixture resembles damp sand.

Measure out ½ cup plus 2 tbsp of the crust mixture and set it aside. Dump the remaining mixture (about 1 ½ cups plus 1/3 cup) into the parchment-lined pan and press the crumbs firmly into an even layer in the bottom of the pan. Place the crust in the oven and bake until firm on top and golden-brown around the edges, 20-25 minutes.

Rhubarb Crumb Bars continued

Meanwhile, return the ½ cup plus 2 tbsp of the crust mixture to the mixing bowl. Add the oats, pecans, brown sugar and flaky salt, mixing to combine, then add the remaining 1 tbsp of butter, in little pieces, mixing until the streusel clumps together and no butter chunks remain.

When the crust has finished baking, spread the jam over the hot crust in an even layer.

Use your fingers to press the streusel mixture into hazelnut-sized clumps and sprinkle it over the top (don't press the streusel into the jam; it should be loose).

Bake the bars until the streusel turns a deep golden brown, 30-35 minutes. Remove from the oven and cool 20 minutes.

Grasp the bottom-most piece of parchment paper by its handles and bravely lift the bar out of the pan and onto a cutting board (it may appear to crack, but will stick back together as it cools). Let cool completely.

Peel away the sides of the parchment (they may stick to the jam). Trim away the outer ¼ inch from each side, then cut into 12 bars.

Notes:
The bars are best the first and second day of baking, when the crust is crisp, but will keep for a few days at room temperature or longer in the 'fridge.

Sticky Toffee Pudding

Richard Nestel, Lantana House B&B

Ingredients:
Pudding:

12 oz finely chopped pitted dates	2 tsp vanilla extract
2 eggs well beaten	2 tsp baking powder
3 ¾ cups all-purpose flour	2 tsp baking soda
1 ¾ cup sugar	4 oz butter (1 stick)
	1 pint boiling water

Topping:
1 cup brown sugar
4 tbsp butter (½ stick)
6 tbsp heavy cream

Directions:
Preheat oven to 375. Grease a 9x9 cake pan.

Cream the butter and sugar. Add eggs to mixture. Add flour, baking soda and baking powder.

Place the dates in another bowl. Add vanilla and boiling water. Combine with the flour mixture.

Pour into prepared pan and bake for 40 minutes.

Topping:
In a sauce pan combine brown sugar, butter and cream. Heat then simmer 'till smooth. Spoon over a slice of pudding and add a dollop of whipped cream.

Satan, Get Thee Back! Chocolate Trifle

Tobey Shepherd, Linden Tree Inn

Ingredients:
1 sm. package instant chocolate pudding mix
2 cups cold milk
2 cups heavy cream
Confectioner's sugar
Shelled hazelnuts, chopped
Chocolate cake or cupcakes, 1 layer or 6 cupcakes
Ghirardelli milk chocolate chips
Ghirardelli dark chocolate chips
Ghirardelli white chocolate chips

Directions:
Make chocolate pudding with 2 cups of whole milk according to directions on package. Take out of mixing bowl.

Pour 2 cups of heavy cream into mixing bowl; no need to wash bowl or beaters - it adds to the flavor! Whip the heavy cream into whipped cream, adding confectioner's sugar to sweeten to your taste. Should be firm enough to hold its shape.

Cut chocolate cake into rough cubes, or just rip into large chunks. Place half of chocolate cake in trifle bowl to cover bottom. Sprinkle with a handful of each flavor of chocolate chips. Cover with a layer of chocolate pudding sprinkled with chopped hazelnuts. Cover with a layer of whipped cream. Follow with a layer of chocolate cake, chips, pudding, nuts and whipped cream.

Decorate the top of the trifle with the 3 types of chocolate chips and chopped hazelnuts. Chill an hour or two before serving.

Notes:
John named this trifle after taking just one bite!!!
I make this for a lot of our retreat groups; it is always a favorite!

Whoopie Pies

Tobey Shepherd, Linden Tree Inn

Ingredients:
6 tbsp Crisco or vegetable shortening
1 cup sugar
1 egg
1 tsp vanilla
1 cup milk
1 tsp salt
2 cups flour
1 ½ tbsp baking soda
5 heaping tbsp cocoa

Filling:
½ cup Crisco
6 heaping tbsp of Marshmallow Fluff
¾ cup confectioner's sugar
Pinch of salt
Milk or half & half

Directions:
To make the cakes:
Preheat oven to 350 degrees. Cream Crisco and sugar, add the egg and vanilla, beat well. Sift dry ingredients together and add alternately with the milk to the creamed ingredients. Drop by spoonful onto ungreased cookie sheets and bake for 12 minutes or until they are done.

To make the filling:
Combine Crisco, confectioner's sugar, Marshmallow Fluff and salt and mix well. Use milk or half & half to thin out the filling so that it will spread.

Match up halves of the cakes and spread filling on one half, cover with the other. Enjoy with a glass of milk!

Notes:
These were always a favorite of my brother's and one year my mother made him a cake with whoopee pies for his birthday! You can make these big or little depending on how big a spoon you use; cooking time will need to be adjusted accordingly.

Fresh Blueberry Pie
Nancy Cameron-Gilsey, The Seaward

Another favorite from The Seaward Inn's classic cookbook, "The Cook's Book – Pierre Tells All!"

Ingredients:
1 quart fresh blueberries
¾ cup water
¼ cup white sugar
¼ cup brown sugar
1 tsp or more lemon juice
¼ tsp salt
Dash cinnamon
3 tbsp cornstarch
¼ cup water
9-inch baked pie shell
Whipped cream

Directions:
Wash and drain 1 quart fresh blueberries. Set aside 3 cups of blueberries in mixing bowl

Combine 1 cup blueberries, crushed, along with ¾ cup water, the white and brown sugar, salt, lemon juice and cinnamon. Cook until soft.

Dissolve the cornstarch in ¼ cup water and add the mixture in slowly.

Cook until thick and clear and boils 3 minutes. Fold into raw blueberries and pour into 9-inch baked pie shell. Chill.

Once cool, top with whipped cream.

Victorian Christmas Pudding

John Shepherd, Linden Tree Inn

See notes below before making and read the recipe all the way through as we have made notations with changes. We made note of our personal favorite substitutions in the ingredients list.

You will need a pudding tin. This is a covered tin that you will put your pudding in to steam. If you do not have a pudding tin or you cannot find one, you can use an oven safe bowl, greased. To cover it we used aluminum foil (grease the side of the aluminum foil that will be against the pudding,) and to secure to the bowl, tied it with cotton twine.

Ingredients:
- 225g/8 oz golden caster sugar (brown sugar is US equivalent)
- 225g/8 oz vegetarian suet, we used Mr. Filberts Golden Quarters
- 120g/4 oz chopped candied peel
- 340g/12 oz sultanas (we used 16 oz mixed dried fruit instead of the sultanas and candied peel)
- 340g/12 oz raisins (we used 8 oz instead of 12 and added 4 oz prunes & dates)
- 225g/8 oz currants
- 120g/4 oz plain flour
- 120g/4 oz fresh white breadcrumbs
- 60g/2 oz flaked almonds (sliced almonds)
- Zest of 1 lemon
- 5 eggs, beaten
- 1 level tsp ground cinnamon
- 1 level tsp mixed spice*
- 1 level tsp freshly grated nutmeg
- Pinch of salt
- 150ml/5 oz brandy or rum

*Mixed spice is equal parts ginger, allspice, cloves, or to your liking.

Victorian Christmas Pudding continued

Directions: In an electric mixer place all the ingredients in the bowl and mix together until all the ingredients are combined. This can be mixed by hand, however the mixture is very stiff.

Place the mixture in the pudding tin (or oven safe bowl) and cover. Prepare your water bath in a pan large enough to steam the pudding tin. The water should come up 2/3 of the way on the pudding tin. Steam for 6 hours. While the pudding is steaming continue to add water to keep it at the level of 2/3 up the tin.

Remove the pudding from the water bath and let cool. Keep the pudding in the tin or bowl until it will be served. It is best to make your pudding around Thanksgiving time, so that it can develop more flavor. A Victorian Pudding lasts a long time and if you "feed" it some brandy every now and again...well, it lasts really well.

On the day of serving, warm up the pudding by re-steaming for 2 hours in a water bath with the water 2/3 way up the side of the tin or bowl. When serving, make it even more special by dousing it in brandy and then lighting it. We serve with whipped cream or vanilla ice cream.

Notes:
This is a recipe that Tobey and I try to make about every year for Christmas. Everyone in the family has to take a turn stirring it to ensure that the next year will bring good fortune.
The recipe is from a British recipe and we added the American equivalents. Everything is measured in weights and we do weigh everything on our kitchen scale for this. I mix it in the Kitchen-Aid mixer. It is a very stiff dough.

Happy Holidays!!

Shalin Liu Performance Center

*Founded in 1981 as the **Rockport Chamber Music Festival**, Rockport Music has been under the artistic direction of violinist/violist Barry Shiffman since 2017. From 1995-2017, the Festival was under the artistic direction of pianist David Deveau. In Summer 2010, the organization completed construction on a year-round permanent home, the Shalin Liu Performance Center. In addition to the Chamber Music Festival, the theater presents live music artists, film festivals and live HD video presentations from the Metropolitan Opera and other renowned theaters. www.rockportmusic.org*

Jams, Jellies & Sauces

Changing Tides
Bed & Breakfast

Rockport Innkeepers Association

Welcome to our updated 1800's home, located in Rockport's historic downtown district.

Our home has three bright and sunny guest rooms, all of which feature skylights. The Captain's Quarters, located at the front of the home, has a queen size bed and a private bath located just outside the door. The Beachcomber Suite, overlooking the gardens in the back yard, has two twin-sized beds that can be converted to a very comfortable king-sized bed and a brand new ensuite bathroom. The Mermaid Suite has a private bathroom with a large walk-in shower with two shower heads and a built-in bench.

We have a large chef's kitchen where your gourmet breakfasts are prepared. The menu changes daily based on the availability of fresh local ingredients and the whims of your hostess and chef, Steph. We will happily meet any special dietary needs with advanced notice. On warm days you can dine outdoors on our screen porch or have your breakfast in the backyard gardens. We have a large living room with a flat screen television and a sitting room where you can chat with Stephanie as she prepares your breakfast.

Just a short walk from the house are three of Rockport's most picturesque beaches; Old Garden Beach, Front Beach and Back Beach. We will provide beach towels, umbrellas and chairs to our guests, should they require them. The famous Bearskin Neck is just a few steps away and is full of quaint shops, colorful galleries and restaurants where fresh seafood is always on the menu.

Changing Tides Bed & Breakfast
Rockport, Massachusetts 01966

Hot Fudge Sauce
Stephanie Smith, Changing Tides Bed &Breakfast

Ingredients:
2/3 cup heavy cream
½ cup light corn syrup
1/3 cup dark brown sugar
¼ cup Dutch processed cocoa powder
¼ tsp sea salt
6 oz bitter sweet chocolate, chopped, divided in half
2 tbsp unsalted better
1 tsp vanilla extract

Directions:
Bring cream, syrup, brown sugar, cocoa powder, salt and half of the chocolate to a boil over medium high heat. Reduce to medium low to simmer for 5 minutes, stirring occasionally.

Remove from heat. Stir in remaining chocolate, butter & vanilla. Stir until smooth. Let cool for 20-30 minutes. It will thicken as it cools.

Store in an air tight container in the refrigerator for up to two weeks.

To reheat, microwave for 30 seconds to 1 minute.

GF

Onion Bacon Jam with Balsamic Vinegar
Stephanie Smith, Changing Tides Bed & Breakfast

Ingredients:
- ¾ pound slab bacon, diced into cubes
- 4 medium-size white or Spanish onions, peeled and diced
- 1 ½ tsp mustard seed
- 2 ½ tbsp dark brown sugar
- ¼ cup balsamic vinegar
- Kosher salt
- Freshly ground black pepper
- 3 tbsp water

Directions:
Set a Dutch oven or heavy pot over medium heat and add the bacon. Cook, stirring occasionally, until the fat is completely rendered and the bacon has started to crisp, approximately 12-15 minutes.

Drain all but 1 tbsp of the fat from the pot and add the onions, mustard seed, brown sugar, vinegar and 3 tbsp of water. Stir to combine then cover the pot, lower the heat and allow the mixture to cook undisturbed for 15 or 20 minutes.

Remove the top, stir again and then partly cover the pot. Allow the mixture to cook until most of the liquid is gone and the onions have achieved a dark brown "jamminess," approximately 60-70 minutes. (Add a little more water as needed.)

GF

Rhubarb Jam

Stephanie Smith, Changing Tides Bed & Breakfast

Ingredients:

1 pound (4-5 large stalks) rhubarb, sliced into ½ inch pieces
¾ cup sugar

Zest and juice of 1 large orange (or 2 small blood oranges)
½ vanilla bean, split lengthwise and scraped

Directions:
In a medium saucepan, combine the ¾ cup sugar, vanilla bean pod and scrapings, orange zest and juice.

Over high heat, bring the mixture to a simmer, then dump in the rhubarb. Cook, stirring frequently, until the mixture has broken down into a thick jam, about 10 minutes. Set aside to cool and remove the vanilla bean. (You can wash it, leave it to dry at room temp and reuse.)

Notes:
Adapted from The Big Sur Bakery Cookbook
Makes 1 ½ cups
The jam can be made up to a week or so ahead. Store in the 'fridge.

GF VG

Stewed Apple-Cranberry Sauce

Scott Wood, Tuck Inn

Ingredients:
4 to 6 apples (depending on size)
½ cup cranberries
½ cup sugar (about)
About 3/4 cup of water
½ tsp cinnamon
1/8 tsp nutmeg

Directions:
(You will need a Foley Food Mill)
Rinse and quarter apples (you don't need to peel or core them).

Combine apples, cranberries and water in covered 2 quart saucepan. Simmer on low heat (stirring occasionally) until apples soften.

Once cooked, put mixture through the Foley Food Mill held over a serving bowl.

Add sugar (sweeten to taste) cinnamon and nutmeg. Mix and serve hot or cold.

Notes:
Tastes particularly good over warm gingerbread.

GF VG

Fudge Sauce
Nancy Cameron-Gilsey, The Seaward

A staple at the Seaward!

Ingredients:
2 tbsp butter	¾ cup sugar
2 squared baker's unsweetened chocolate	¾ cup evaporated milk
	1 tsp vanilla

Directions:
Melt the butter and chocolate. Add the sugar and evaporated milk. Cook slowly until smooth and graininess disappears. Add the vanilla.

Makes about one cup. Store in the refrigerator.

GF

Benjamin Tarr House – 1630
Answering a sudden alarm to meet at the house of Lieutenant Benjamin Tarr, grandson of Richard Tarr the first settler, sixty-six men from this village, under Captain John Rowe, marched to Charlestown and fought in the Battle of Bunker Hill. The house still stands on South Street.

Roasted Tomato Sauce for Canning

Stephanie Smith, Changing Tides Bed & Breakfast

Ingredients:
About 7 lbs tomatoes
4 or 5 cloves of sliced garlic
2 tsp EVOO
3 ¼ tsp other salt
4 tsp sugar
2 tbsp EVOO

Directions:
Preheat oven to 450.

In large bowl toss tomatoes with 2 tsp EVOO and 1 tsp salt.

Line sheet pan with foil and roast tomatoes and garlic for 1 hour.

Transfer roasted tomatoes to food mill or food processor and blend.

Place tomatoes in large sauce pot adding remaining salt, sugar and EVOO. You can add basil & oregano if you want and if you want it a bit spicy you can add hot pepper flakes.

Can at 11 lbs for 15 mins.

GF VG

Spiced Crock-Pot Apple Butter for Canning
Stephanie Smith, Changing Tides Bed & Breakfast

Ingredients:
5 lbs apples (peeled, cored & sliced)
2 cup brown sugar
2 cup white sugar
1 cup apple cider
2 tsp cinnamon
½ tsp allspice
¼ tsp cloves
¼ tsp nutmeg
¼ tsp salt
Sometimes I add a tbsp fresh grated ginger for extra spice

Directions:
Peel, core and slice all of the apples and place them in the crock-pot.

In a separate bowl, combine the sugars, spices and salt. Pour the mixture over the apples and stir well, making sure to coat all of the apples. Add the cider.

Place crock-pot on low and cook for 10-12 hours (I do overnight). After the 10-12 hours, mash any chunks of apple that remain. Allow to cook for an additional two hours.

Remove the lid and use an immersion blender to blend the apple butter until it's smooth. If you prefer, you can let the apple butter cook a little longer with the lid slightly ajar to let it thicken up some more.

GF VG

Hollandaise Sauce

Sawsan Galal, Sally Webster Inn

Ingredients:
3 egg yolks
1 tsp water
12 tbsp (1 ½ sticks) unsalted butter, chilled and cut into small pieces
¼ tsp sugar
½ tsp kosher salt
2 tsp freshly squeezed lemon juice
1/8 tsp cayenne pepper

Directions:
Pour 1-inch of water into a large saucepan; over medium heat, bring to a simmer. Once simmering, reduce the heat to low.

Place egg yolks and 1 tsp water in a medium mixing bowl and whisk until mixture lightens in color, approximately 1 to 2 minutes. Add the sugar and whisk for another 30 seconds.

Place the mixture over the simmering water and whisk constantly for 3 to 5 minutes or until there is a clear line that is drawn in the mixture when you pull your whisk through or the mixture coats the back of a spoon.

Remove the bowl from over the pan and gradually add the butter, 1 piece at a time and whisk until all of the butter is incorporated.

Place the bowl back over the simmering water occasionally so that it will be warm enough the melt the butter. Add the salt, lemon juice and cayenne pepper.

Serve immediately or hold in a thermos to keep warm.

GF

Bearnaise Sauce

Sawsan Galal, Sally Webster Inn

Ingredients:

3 tbsp white wine
3 tbsp white vinegar
¼ crushed peppercorn
½ tsp dry tarragon or 2 sprigs of fresh tarragon

1 small shallot, chopped
1 stick butter, melted
2 egg yolks
1 tbsp water
Salt and pepper to taste

Directions:

In a saucepan, combine the wine, vinegar, peppercorns, shallots and tarragon. Bring the liquid to a boil and reduce to 1 tbsp. Add 1 tbsp of water.

Strain and combine the reduced liquid and egg yolks in a stainless bowl, over simmering water. Whisk until frothy.

In a steady stream, add the butter until the sauce thickens. Season with salt and pepper.

Strain the sauce through a chinois and set aside.

GF

Cape Ann Plein Air
For one week in October, forty Plein Air (outdoor) artists are invited from across the globe to beautiful Cape Ann, to capture scenes of Rockport, Gloucester, Essex and Manchester-by-the-Sea. These modern masters will set out to work from nature, in Cape Ann's great Plein Air painting tradition. You can watch them work, celebrate their remarkable paintings and seize the chance to own a piece of original art! www.capeannpleinair.com

Easy Raspberry Sauce
Sawsan Galal, Sally Webster Inn

Ingredients
2 cups fresh or frozen raspberries
1/3 cup sugar
1 ¾ cups plus 1 tbsp water, divided
2 tbsp cornstarch

Directions
In a saucepan, combine the raspberries, 1 ¾ cups water and sugar. Bring to a boil. Reduce heat; simmer, uncovered, for 30 minutes.

Mash raspberry mixture and strain through a fine sieve into a 2 cup measuring cup; discard seeds. Add water if needed to make 2 cups puree. Return to the saucepan.

Combine cornstarch and remaining water until smooth; gradually stir into raspberry mixture. Bring to a boil over medium heat, stirring constantly. Cook and stir 1 minute longer. Remove from the heat; cool. Store in the refrigerator.

Notes:
Great on pancakes or waffles or on ice cream!

GF

Odds & Ends

The Seaward

A slice of heaven in Rockport...

The Seaward, offers charming seaside vacation rentals weekly, (or nightly during the shoulder seasons.) Our property offers a variety of accommodations including Gap Cove (two bedroom, two bath apartment), Spruces (cozy two bedroom cottage with working fireplace) Gully Point and Loblolly Cove (one bedroom suites with spectacular deck views) and Lover's Cove (featuring a king bedroom with private garden seating). Relax and unwind with coastal breezes, the sight of soaring gulls and sounds of gentle waves on the rocks.

Stroll to the beach along The Old Garden Path and continue to The Headlands, with a breathtaking vista of the ocean and town. Enjoy a glass of wine in our beautiful grounds and gardens. Cruise into nearby downtown for fresh lobster, entertainment, great shopping and recreational activities. Or simply enjoy a sunset on the ocean from your deck or patio.

A review from a recent guest:
"The Seaward is a very relaxing, peaceful location. The accommodations were very clean and comfortable. We had a cute front deck with rocking chairs to sit and watch the breathtaking ocean views. We rode up from Boston by train...Nancy picked us up from the train station and gave us a tour of Rockport by car. We were given bicycles to get around the village. I can't tell you how much fun we had...highly recommended."

All of our cottage and apartment rentals have a kitchen area, Wi-Fi and an ocean view! A favorite Rockport vacation rental, come experience all that is The Seaward.

The Seaward
42 Marmion Way, Rockport, Massachusetts 01966
508-284-2468
seaward.rockport@gmail.com
www.theseawardrockport.com

Maple Syrup Salad Dressing
Nancy Cameron-Gilsey, The Seaward

Ingredients:
4 tbsp pure maple syrup
1 tbsp Dijon mustard
¼ cup apple cider vinegar
3/4 cup EVOO
¼ tsp black pepper or to taste
¼ tsp salt or to taste

Directions:
Whisk all ingredients together and enjoy!

GF

Mint Vinaigrette Dressing
Sawsan Galal, Sally Webster Inn

Ingredients:
¼ cup red wine vinegar
¾ cup olive oil
1 tsp (or less) salt
Pepper to taste
2 tsp crushed dry mint leaves
½ tsp garlic powder

Directions:
Place in a jar and shake well.
Yields 1 cup.

GF VG

House Pickles
The Emerson Inn

Ingredients:

Pickling cucumbers, washed and sliced thin
Garlic, sliced
White vinegar
Salt
Sugar
Pickling spice
Fresh dill, chopped
Red chili flake
Water

Directions:
In a pot, prepare the pickling brine use the following ratio
- 1 part water
- 3 parts vinegar
- ½ part salt
- ¼ part sugar

Add 2 oz pickling spice and 2 oz chili flake, to the pot and bring to a boil.

While the brine is heating up place cucumbers in bowl with sliced garlic and chopped dill.

Once liquid is at a rapid boil carefully remove from heat and strain out the pickling spice. Pour hot liquid over the cucumbers, weigh them down with a pan and allow them to cool.

GF VG

Laura's Grilled Corn Salsa

Chris & Beth Roenker, Seafarer Inn

We always ask our sister-in-law, Laura to bring her corn salsa. This dish has appeared at many outdoor dinner parties in the Roenker family. A perennial favorite!

Ingredients:
4 ears of corn, shucked	½ medium red onion, chopped
Olive oil for brushing the corn	2 tbsp chopped fresh cilantro
1 ripe large tomato, chopped	1 tbsp fresh lime juice
	Salt to taste

Directions:
Light a charcoal grill and when red hot, brush the corn with olive oil and place on the grill. Allow the corn to cook on the cob and even to char a little for color. Remove when cooked and allow to cool.

Cut the kernels from the cobs and place in a large bowl. Add the remaining ingredients and adjust the seasoning as needed.

Enjoy!

Notes:
I confess, sometimes we use a gas grill, but we know charcoal tastes better!
If you like to plan ahead, add a few extra ears of corn to the grill on one day and use the leftovers for the salsa the next day.

GF VG

Remoulade Tartar Sauce
Helene and Dan Duffy, The Beech Tree B&B

Ingredients:
1 cup Mayonnaise
½ cup honey mustard
1/8 cup cocktail sauce
½ minced red pepper
½ minced green pepper
½ minced yellow pepper
1 Tbsp Tabasco
¼ cup minced celery

Directions:
Mix all ingredients in a bowl and keep chilled.

Serve with crab cakes, shrimp, fried clams or any crispy fish.

Notes:
Ingredient amounts can be changed to your particular taste.

Moroccan Spice Blend (Ras El Hanout)
Sawsan Galal, Sally Webster Inn

Ingredients:
½ tsp aniseed
1 tsp fennel seeds
8 whole allspice berries
Seeds from 8 cardamom pods
8 whole cloves
15 whole black peppercorns
1 stick cinnamon, broken in half

1 tbsp sesame seeds
1 tsp coriander seeds
½ tsp cumin seed
Pinch dried red pepper flakes
1 tbsp ground ginger
1 tsp freshly ground nutmeg

Directions:
Combine all ingredients and keep in an airtight container.

This blend can be used with meats as a rub or in meat or veggie stews as a seasoning. It is very aromatic.

GF VG

Chai Recipe
Sawsan Galal, Sally Webster Inn

This is my secret blend for the best Chai!

Ingredients:
2 tbsp cinnamon
2 tbsp ginger
1 tbsp cardamom

1 tbsp ground cloves
1 tbsp black pepper
4 tbsp black tea

Enjoy!

GF VG

Elizabeth's Famous Power Balls

Nancy Cameron-Gilsey, The Seaward

Ingredients:
Power Balls:
½ cup almond butter
1/3 cup maple syrup
1 ½ cup old-fashioned rolled oats
¼ cup sliced almonds
¼ cup dried, unsweetened tart cherries or blueberries
¼ cup raw, shelled pumpkin seeds

Toppings:
½ cup hemp seeds, unsweetened coconut or wheat germ

Directions:
In a large bowl, combine the almond butter and maple syrup. Mix with an electric mixer until completely combined. With mixer on low, gradually add the oats until incorporated. Add remaining Power Ball ingredients and mix on low until just combined.

Line a baking sheet with wax paper or parchment paper.

For each ball, use a tablespoon to take a heaping scoop of the mixture and, with your hands, gently roll into a ball. (I use a mini ice cream scoop.)

Roll each ball in the hemp seeds, coconut or wheat germ and set on the lined baking sheet.

Refrigerate the baking sheet for a couple of hours; then transfer the power balls to a container and store in the 'fridge for up to 2 weeks or freeze for up to six months. (They won't spoil in the freezer but may acquire that dreaded "freezer taste".)

Elizabeth's Famous Power Balls continued

Notes:
I have seriously messed with this recipe and had great luck. I made a peanut butter chocolate version with the following substitutions:

Peanut butter in place of the almond butter. Add 3 tbsp organic cacao powder. Keep the cherries or switch out for minced raisins Add ¼ cup mini dark chocolate chips.

When I made them with peanut butter, they were a bit drier, maybe because of the cacao powder. When I made the balls, I used wet hands to roll them and the problem was solved. I also rolled this version in finely crushed, salted roasted peanuts.

I have also added in a couple of pinches of cardamom to the blueberry version and ¼ teaspoon of cinnamon to the dried cherry version.

Play with the recipe, subbing other nuts or seeds, making sure they are small enough to allow rolling the appropriate size ball.

Bacon in the Oven
Chris Roenker, Seafarer Inn

We make bacon every morning. We've tried a few methods and settled on this one. Perfect every time.

Directions:
Preheat oven to 400.
Line two rimmed baking sheets with aluminum foil.

Separate one pound of bacon onto the two pans. Bacon should not overlap.

Place one pan on each of two racks in the midsection of the oven and set timer to 7 minutes. At 7 minutes, rotate the pans so the bottom is on the top and the top moves to the bottom of the two racks. Cook for 7 more minutes.

Remove bacon to a paper towel-lined plate to drain the fat.

GF

Christmas in Rockport
The Christmas Season is bustling in Rockport. Each weekend, you will find holiday events for the whole family. Santa arrives by lobster boat the first Saturday of December and lights the Town Tree while the whole town sings carols. Enjoy a gallery stroll, crafters' sales, carriage rides, special shopping, beautiful lights, window displays and concert events and, on the last Saturday of the month, a live nativity Pageant. On Christmas morning, Santa returns to Dock Square for a personal visit with the children of Rockport. www.rockportusa.com/events-festivals

Balsamic Reduction Gastrique
Helene Duffy, The Beech Tree B&B

Two of our very first guests were accomplished chefs and New Hampshire restauranteurs who specialize in locally sourced farm to table menus and fresh fish. They quickly became friends and actually reversed roles, cooking us a delicious Sea Bass dinner in our kitchen served with this reduction sauce. We loved it so much we've adapted it for other dishes as well. It's yummy on roasted Brussels sprouts.

Ingredients:
1 bottle balsamic vinegar (use a good brand)
1 cup sugar
1-2 tbsp orange juice
Black pepper to taste
A few springs of fresh thyme
1 tsp grated lemon peel

Directions:
Combine and simmer ingredients about an hour until it reduces into half the amount and coats a spoon.

Use it as a sauce for fresh fish. It can be refrigerated for another use and time.

Notes:
While simmering the scent of the vinegar will pervade the kitchen so be prepared!

Rockport New Year's Eve
Join the crowd in downtown Rockport for over 40 different shows and events; musical events, dancing, children's shows and a great party ending in the ball dropping in Dock Square to welcome the New Year! www.rockportnye.org

Irresistible **Christmas Candy**
Tobey Shepherd, Linden Tree Inn

Ingredients:
35 saltine crackers
2 sticks unsalted butter
1 cup packed brown sugar
1 ¾ cups semisweet chocolate chips
1 bag red and green M&Ms
1 jar sprinkles of any kind
1/3 cup marshmallows (optional)

Directions:
Preheat oven to 350 degrees. Line a baking sheet or jelly roll pan with tin foil and coat with cooking spray. Line the foiled baking sheet with saltine crackers and set aside

In medium saucepan melt butter and brown sugar and bring to a boil, stirring continuously for about 2 minutes. Pour mixture over crackers in an even layer and bake for 5-6 minutes.

Top with chocolate chips and bake for another 3 minutes or until melted.

Top with M&Ms and sprinkles and marshmallows if you are using them.

Cut into squares and then cool till chocolate is hardened.

Notes:
So tasty you won't want to stop eating it!!!
I like using the sprinkles that come in different shapes and were all mixed up in one jar. You can adapt this for any occasion by changing out the colors of the M&Ms and sprinkles!

The Inns of Rockport Cookbook

Index

Pleasant Street Inn

The Pleasant Street Inn is a Victorian inn situated on a knoll overlooking the village. One can enjoy the peace and quiet of Rockport with the convenience of staying just a short walk from the beaches, restaurants, art galleries and shops.

The Inn has retained the architectural integrity of this home while providing modern conveniences to make your stay more enjoyable.

Each of the eight rooms, furnished for your maximum comfort, has a private bathroom. The hearty breakfast features homemade muffins, a warm entrée, fruit, yogurt, cereals, plus warm and cold drinks, and is served in the dining room. Guests are invited to relax in the cozy living room and to experience the large front porch taking in the views of the landscaped grounds accented by ocean breezes.

Wi-Fi is free and available throughout the Inn. A computer for our guests and a television are found in the living room. Ample parking is available.

Not only does the Inn offer Bed and Breakfast accommodations for overnight stays, but a Carriage House Apartment and a Cottage are available for your longer family vacation.

One will find an inviting, casual atmosphere at the Pleasant Street Inn.

Pleasant Street Inn
17 Pleasant Street, Rockport, Massachusetts 01966

Index

Breads & Muffins	9	GF = Gluten Free VG = Vegan
Anadama Bread	34	
Apple Cider Doughnuts	23	
Banana Muffins	21	GF VG
Banana Bread, Fool Proof	51	
Blueberry Coffee Cake	15	
Blueberry Scones	11	
Blueberry-Nut Muffins	12	
Buttermilk Corn Bread	50	
Cinnamon Rolls, No Yeast	44	
Coffee Cake Basic Mix	52	
Corn Toasties or Muffins	13	
Cranberry Coffee Cake	14	
Cranberry Apple Walnut Bread	22	
French Apple Cake	47	
French Apple Cake Gluten Free	48	GF
Fruit and Nut Bread	24	
Fudgy Chocolate Muffins	20	GF VG
Lemon Bread	25	
Lemon Nut Bread	26	
Maple Walnut Scones	27	
Mary Richardson's Irish Bread	28	
Oatmeal Breakfast Bread	49	GF
Oatmeal Pecan Muffins	29	
Popovers	32	
Pumpkin Bread	30	
Pumpkin Spice Cake Gluten Free	42	GF
Pumpkin Spice Muffins	46	
Rhubarb Streusel Bread	31	
Rhubarb Streusel Coffee Cake	40	
Rhubarb Streusel Muffins	39	
Rich Biscuits	36	
Scones, Pumpkin	18	
Scones, Tobey's Melt-in-your-Mouth	16	
Sweet Muffins	37	
Sour Cream Coffee Cake	19, 33	
Wisconsin Apple Bread	38	

Fruits & Smoothies	55	
4th of July Fun with Fruit	59	GF VG
Poached Pears	58	GF
Roasted Mascarpone Peaches	57	GF
Smoothies:	60	
Banana Split	61	
Berry Twist	61	
Blueberry & Orange	64	
Breakfast Energy	60	
Fall Fashion	62	
Good Morning Sunshine	62	
Mango & Coconut Shakeup	63	GF
Mango Raspberry Smoothie	64	
Mid-day Delight	63	GF VG
Orange Julius	60	
Pineapple Pleasure	65	
Purple Pineapple	65	

Cereals & Yogurts	67	
Granola, Lantana House	69	GF
Granola, Maple Pecan	73	GF VG
Granola, Orange Zest	70	GF VG
Granola, Tuck Inn	72	GF VG
Hot Quinoa Cereal	74	GF VG
Overnight Oats	75	GF
Yogurt Parfait Bar	76	GF

Savory Breakfasts	77	
Avocado Toast	79	
Bacon in the Oven	254	
Cape Hedge Sunrise	87	
Egg Baskets	93	GF
Eggs Benedict/Oscar/Florentine	84	
Frittata, Asparagus & Crab	82	
Frittata, Zucchini	80	GF
Ham & Egg Pepper Rings	89	
Layered Hash Brown Pie	94	GF
Noodle Pudding	97	
Oven Souffle' Savory	130	
Puffed Eggs	88	
Quiche, Asparagus, Mushroom, Ham	98	
Quiche, Crabmeat	96	
Quiche, Easy Crustless Basic	100	GF
Quiche, Tomato Basil Crustless	92	GF
Scrambled Egg Casserole	90	

Summer Squash & Ricotta Casserole	101	
Sundried Tomato, Potato Hash	86	GF
Sweet Breakfasts	**103**	
Almond Croissants	120	
Apple Dumplings	106	
Blueberry Bread Pudding	107	
Bread Pudding w/ Pear Sauce	128	
Crepe, Basic	122	
Crepe, Strawberry Cream	122	
Dutch Babies	130	
French Toast, Chris' Famous	111	
French Toast, Crème Brulee	114	
French Toast, Pecan Praline	112	
French Toast, Pineapple	116	
Orange Marmalade Yoghurt Cake	118	
Pancakes, Blueberry	108	
Pancakes, Lemon Ricotta	109	
Pancakes, Pumpkin Ginger	110	
Peach Oat Crisp	216	
Waffles	105, 125	
Waffles, Chocolate GF VG	124	GF VG
Waffles, Gluten Free and Vegan	123	GF VG
Waffles, Peaches and Cream	126	
Appetizers	**133**	
Artichoke Dip	142	GF
Carrot and Toasted Almond Dip	140	GF VG
Cheese Logs	144	
Cheese Balls, Cranberry Pecan	145	
Feta Tomato Dip	143	
Kielbasa with BBQ Glaze	141	
Party Rye with Cheese	135	
Smoked Bluefish Pate'	137	
Spanish Meatballs	138	
Spicy Shrimp	136	GF
Soups	**147**	
Basic Broth, Chicken or Vegetable	152	
Beef Barley Soup	159	
Butternut Squash Bisque	149	GF
Celery Root Potato Soup	151	GF
Chicken Soup, Thai Style	154	
Chicken Taco Soup	160	
Chilled Mango Cucumber Soup	150	GF VG

Clam Chowder	155	
Coconut Curry Soup	161	
Corn Chowder	158	
Cream of Broccoli, Vegan	153	GF VG
Cream of Tomato Soup	156	
Main Dishes	**163**	
Poultry:		
Bolognese Sauce	166	
Chicken & Lentil Casserole	169	
Chicken Sandwiches	172	
Chicken Stew	168	
Chicken Stuffed with Spinach	170	GF
Taco Casserole	167	
Meat and Pork:		
Beef Tenderloin	176	GF
Cincinnati Chili	174	
Chili con Carne	173	
Ham Asparagus Quiche	98	
Meatloaf, Roly Poly	183	
Meatloaf, Stephanie's Favorite	184	
Pot Roast	178	
Shepherd's Pie	165	GF
Swedish Meatballs	179	
Seafood:		
Aglio with Clams	186	
Baked Haddock	189	
Boiled Lobster	190	GF
Crab Cakes with Tarragon Cr	188	
Crab Quiche	96	
Scallops with Red Pepper Cr	187	
Vegetarian:		
Easy Baked Macaroni & Cheese	181	
Macaroni and Cheese	180	
Pastierre	182	
Salads & Sides	**191**	
Salads:		
Cantaloupe and Cucumber Salad	197	GF
Cucumber Salad	194	GF VG
Grilled Caesar Salad	195	
Mixed Grain Salad	201	GF VG
Potato Salad	193	GF
Roasted Beet Salad	198	

Side Dishes:		
Boston Baked Beans	200	
Corn Pudding	199	
Cous Cous	203	
Holiday Vegetable Mix	196	GF VG
Spicy Potatoes	202	GF VG
Desserts	**205**	
Apple Cake	214	
Apple Crisp	213	
Apple Dumplings	106	
Baklava	218	
Blueberry Pie	229	
Chocolate Pie	217	
Crème Brulee	207, 210	GF
Chocolate Mousse	208	GF
Chocolate Streusel Bars	221	
Chocolate Trifle	227	
French Apple Cake	47	
Kahlua Cake	209	
Lemon Bars	222	
Mango & Coconut Shakeup	63	VG
Oatmeal Apple Cookies	223	GF
Peach Oat Crisp	216	
Peanut Butter Pie	217	
Pecan Pie	220	
Rhubarb Crumb Bars	224	
Roasted Mascarpone Peaches	57	GF
Sticky Toffee Pudding	226	
Strawberry Rhubarb Crisp	212	
Victorian Christmas Pudding	230	
Whoopie Pies	228	
Jams, Jellies & Sauces	**233**	
Apple Butter for Canning	241	GF VG
Apple-Cranberry Sauce	238	GF VG
Béarnaise Sauce	243	GF
Fudge Sauce	239	GF
Hollandaise Sauce	242	GF
Hot Fudge Sauce	235	GF
Onion Bacon Jam w Balsamic	236	GF
Raspberry Sauce	244	GF
Rhubarb Jam	237	GF VG
Tomato Sauce for Canning	240	GF VG

Odds & Ends	245	
Bacon in the Oven	254	GF
Balsamic Reduction	255	
Chai Recipe	251	GF VG
Christmas Candy	256	
Grilled Corn Salsa	249	GF VG
House Pickles	248	GF VG
Maple Syrup Dressing	247	GF
Moroccan Spice Blend	251	GF VG
Power Balls	252	
Remoulade Tartar Sauce	250	
Vinaigrette Dressing	247	GF VG

"The Inns of Rockport Cookbook" is available on Amazon.com. Wholesale rates available upon request (minimum order 10.) Contact: bethcheney@verizon.net

About The Rockport Innkeepers Association

Members of The Rockport Innkeepers Association work together to share information and marketing, and to promote Rockport as a favorite vacation destination. Each member Inn is individually owned and operated. They work hard and take great pleasure in providing top quality accommodations in order to give their guests a memorable stay on Cape Ann in beautiful Rockport, Massachusetts. www.innsofrockport.com

Plan your escape today.   One day is not enough.

Members of the Rockport Innkeepers Association:

Addison Choate	addisonchoate.com
Beech Tree B&B	beechtreebb.com
Cottages by the Sea	rockportvacationhomes.com
The Cove at Rockport	coveatrockport.com
Eagle House Motel	eaglehousemotel.com
Eden Pines Inn	edenpinesinn.com
Emerson Inn	emersoninnbythesea.com
Lantana House B&B	thelantanahouse.com
Periwinkle Cottage	anextrabedvacationrentals.com
Rockport Cottages	rockportcottages.com
Rockport Inn & Suites	rockportinnandsuites.com
Sally Webster Inn	sallywebster.com
The Seafarer Inn	seafarer-inn.com
Seven South Street Inn	sevensouthstreetinn.com
The Seaward	theseasardrockport.com
The Yankee Clipper Inn	yankeeclipperinn.com

About Our Artists

David Arsenault was born in upstate New York. He was first captivated by art in 1970 when he discovered a reproduction of Edward Hopper's painting *Gas* in a grade school library book. However, it wasn't until the early '90s—more than twenty years later—that a professor in his graphic arts program reintroduced him to Hopper's work and he felt compelled to study painting. The early influence had its effect on him to the degree that *The Wall Street Journal* once wrote that "Some of Mr. Arsenault's paintings could pass for works by Edward Hopper."

He studied painting at the University at Albany (NY). Since he first began showing his work in 1993, David has had or participated in hundreds of local, regional, and national exhibitions: in New York City, Chicago, Cape Cod and Martha's Vineyard in Massachusetts, and in Vermont, Connecticut, and of course throughout upstate New York. Arsenault has also served as an exhibition juror, conducted painting demonstrations and critiques, and published articles. He is also former co-director of the Schenectady New York Oakroom Artists, one of the oldest membership-by-invitation artist associations in the United States. His oil paintings, giclée prints, and reproductions are found in private and corporate collections all across the United States, as well as around the world.

He and his wife Rev. Sue Koehler-Arsenault relocated to the seaside town of Rockport, Massachusetts in November 2014 with the goal of opening a gallery. On March 27, 2015 they opened The Art of David Arsenault on Bearskin Neck. David was juried into the renowned Rockport Art Association & Museum in early 2016.

The Gallery relocated to its current location at 8 Dock Square in Rockport on December 1, 2016. Housed in an historic 1740 building, the gallery is also a working studio where you can meet the artist and experience the beauty and peace of your favorite Cape Ann places in David's colorful, dramatically-lit paintings and fine art prints.

You can follow David and the gallery on Facebook at his page, The Art of David Arsenault, and on Instagram. But a visit to Rockport, one of New England's most beautiful towns, is by far the best way to see for yourself.

About Our Artists

Lauri Kaihlanen is a second generation Finnish-American. Lauri combines his amazing draftsmanship with subtle design techniques to entice the eye and engage the heart. His art mirrors his whimsical sense of humor and love of exuberant color. He began drawing and painting as a very young boy using athletics and the Cape Ann, Massachusetts waterfront as his subjects. He attended the New England School of Art, earned a Bachelor of Arts degree at Massachusetts College of Art and a Bachelor of Science Degree in Education at Salem State College. After teaching art in public schools for several years, he left teaching in order to devote full time to his painting. Over the years, Lauri's work has evolved from purely representational through abstract fantasy, back to representational subject matter which floats on abstract backgrounds. Lauri's unusual style incorporates traditional painting techniques and disparate subjects, combined with distinct abstract concepts including collage, montage and heavy over-painting. The artist paints in acrylic on illustration board.

Lauri has owned his own gallery for over twenty years. He has been commissioned by several restaurants on Captiva Island, Florida creating the artwork which uniquely captured the essence of the space and style of the restaurants. 'Tween Waters Resort on Captiva Island owns several of Lauri's paintings and displays them in their Crow's Nest Restaurant. Lauri has been commissioned by many residents of Captiva and Sanibel Islands to paint local scenes and especially Florida's wildlife. These commissions include a large mural painted across an entire wall of a new house. He was commissioned to paint a large piece for the International Fund for Animal Welfare, (IFAW) a worldwide organization dedicated to promoting the just and kind treatment of animals and to preserving animals from extinction. Ocean Reef Resort, in Key Largo, Florida commissioned Lauri to paint eighteen large wooden pieces which now hang in their recreational center. Lauri's work continues to be collected by devoted followers worldwide.

Lauri's works can be seen at Kaihlanen Galleries on historic Bearskin Neck in Rockport or you can follow him on Facebook on his page, Lauri Kaihlanen Gallery.

Rockport Innkeepers Association

Shop Small – Shop Local

We encourage our guests to book directly through the B&B, Hotel or Inn's website or by phone and to avoid unaffiliated on-line travel agencies.

By Shopping Small and Booking Direct, you will find:

- more accurate and complete information regarding room types and amenities
- more accurate and complete information about the house such as location and type of lodging
- more choices of available rooms

On-line Travel Agencies:

- may not list our information completely or correctly
- often highlight one room, preventing you from seeing your choices
- often incorrectly show an inn to be full when it has vacancy
- always charge the B&B or Inn a percentage of the room rate

Shop Small! Shop Local!
Book Direct!

Made in the USA
Middletown, DE
05 March 2023